"WHEN YOUR DREA
WORST N.......MARE

DOOMED IN
DUBAI

NADEEM AHMED

Acknowledgements

I would really like to thank everyone who has supported me throughout my career and believed in me and my potential to excel especially my beautiful family members and my amazing friends who are my family. Thank you all for putting up with my mood swings and off days and continuously supporting me through thick and thin. I would not have achieved anything without your love and support. It means the world to me. I want you all to know that you will always be part of my success. I don't need to write individual names, you all know exactly who you are.

Thanks a million, love you all loads xxx

Contents

DISCLAIMER

Some of the character names and descriptions have been changed due to legal reasons and some have remained the same with permission from the people involved.

CHAPTER 1

It's a wrap,' shouted the photographer in a relieved tone. In all fairness, it had been quite a long day. So many different outfits to wear, so many different looks! Hair scraped back, then put forward, then spiked and the tortured look on my face as makeup was plastered on to the max to enhance my already chiselled look. Pose, pout, pose, pout all day long. Not to forget the long-held smiles that literally hurt my face after a while. Who said being a model was easy?

I can't deny that I loved my job. I met so many different beautiful characters from all walks of life and had the opportunity to travel to all sorts of weird and wonderful locations, whether it was a dilapidated alleyway, or a cute little cottage in the middle of a field in the middle of nowhere. I guess this added to the excitement of not knowing where I was going to be, how I would get there or what I would be doing on my next assignment. This most certainly went against all rules of working in an office, something I would never be able to handle!

I lived in a tiny town called Accrington where the grass is a beautiful shade of green, and the houses are cute and full of character. However, the size of my childhood place was so small that everyone knew everyone's business to the extent of who was doing what where and when. Naturally, being the black sheep of my family and community I didn't follow the so called conventional trends, for example becoming a doctor, accountant or a dentist. I had always felt fuelled to look in the complete opposite direction. I had come to terms with the fact that I was a creative and would never be a technical person a long time ago. It was common knowledge in Accrington that I was a model. My pictures were on display all over the world and I was making a good living from it, however it just wasn't considered a real career to anyone. People did not understand the fact that there was a certain art to becoming a model and it was not easy work. This was the ugly negative attitude that gave me the ultimate push to excel and take my career to the ultimate heights.

Tuesday 23rd December 2003. What a great way to begin the week and end it at the same time by completing my final project of the year. What a year it had been! I had worked extremely hard, without a doubt, doing literally about four shoots a week, sometimes five, each job taking me all over the country.

Even though I may not have shown it I was exhausted and so in desperate need of a break to switch off. Thank God Christmas was soon upon us. I had always been a huge fan of Christmas and loved all the trimmings that came with it. It was the only time of year where the whole family got together to enjoy quality time and the huge banquet that was always laid out. It was impossible to make any lame excuses for not meeting up too! Like most people I loved and appreciated my food and always looked forward to stuffing my face. At this time of year, I broke the entire rules full pelt. On a normal day, I would never eat anything fried or greasy, for example chips, or samosas etc. It was either grilled or raw. I had always been disciplined. A prime example was when I used to visit my aunt's house which was about fifteen minutes away. She would always make meat rolls and samosas. This was her speciality and no doubt tasted divine, however she would fry them freshly right in front of me which made it worse as I could smell the scrumptious smell and watch everyone else crunch through the precisely folded parcels. Both the smell and crunch would be magnified by a million times and I would be left dribbling at the mouth literally. I had no choice but to resist because of work. No pain no gain!

Working away a lot meant not seeing any of my friends or family for a long time which was definitely a downside to the modelling life. All my cousins were growing up so quickly. I felt I was missing out on them transitioning from a child to adulthood. At least I had the family reunion at Christmas to look forward to which would be the perfect opportunity to catch up on all the latest gossip.

I hated the cold and if I had a choice of living in extreme heat or extreme cold there would be no question of me residing in a hotter climate. We always had the worst of winters up north. What frustrated me about winter was the fact you had to layer up in so many garments. I mean how could one look fashionable looking like the Michelin Man? The snow may have looked like a pure clean white blanket covering the village but it was the aftermath we had to pay for like black ice and lack of transport - not that there was much transport at the best of times. If you missed your train or bus by 11pm then you are sure to be stranded. Thankfully I drove. In those days, my car was an essential tool to get to work due to my strange schedule.

My bag was like something out of Mary Poppins, full of shoes, accessories, deodorant sprays and everything else you can think of that would be required for a shoot. I didn't have the energy to place it nicely in the back of my car so I threw it in.

I was so tired I couldn't be bothered to even wash my face but then I was driving home so no-one was going to see me in my full glory. Even if they did I didn't care. Luckily, I had been working in Manchester city centre so the drive home was going to be roughly about thirty minutes. No more work till the New Year yeahhhhh!!! I could eat drink and be merry.

It must have been my lucky day, I seemed to have missed all the traffic and got home quicker than normal. I lived with my grandparents and my younger brother lived with my mum just a short distance away. My sister was married and lived in her own home just a short walk away too. That was the beauty of living in such a small town; the fact that everything was just a short distance away. By now most of my family had got used to the idea that I was a creative individual and too stubborn to do anything else. Some of them took to it well whereas others thought I was wasting my time and a no hoper in life. Unfortunately, you can choose your friends but not your family! When younger I always used to think my family were so perfect. When I got older I realised we were no longer the Walton's. Maybe they were just simply jealous because I was making a name for myself on a worldwide scale which I guess is not abnormal. It was always the people closest to you that were happy to put you down any given opportunity!

Finally, I was through the front door and raced towards the cosy couch where I comfortably passed out for what seemed like a long time. It wasn't long enough, an hour maximum. I was awoken by my very beautiful grandmother, my second mum, a very elegant lady who like me was a social butterfly. A very sensitive and loved filled soul who cried at anything on television that showed cruelty to any human beings be it a child or adult! It's not surprising she was well known throughout the town for her kindness and generosity. As always, she had prepared a delicious dinner for me. Chicken curry in thick spicy sauce accompanied by freshly made chapattis (home made fresh bread). My favourite! Having eaten a very healthy portion the thought of collapsing on my bed seemed like a very tempting idea however I wasn't going to be unsociable so I decided to freshen up and head out to my sisters with my grandmother as the masses (my family) were coming to spend a few days with us. Naturally I was looking forward to seeing some of them, if not all!

After a long night of eating, chatting and more eating at my sisters it was time to get up and have a reality check. Time to go home and put away the model and bring out the domesticated me! The yellow marigolds were screaming out my name loudly which meant it was that dreaded time for a full-on spring clean. Scrubbing, washing, dusting, and vacuuming.

Exciting times! God, it seemed to take forever. Miraculously it was all done within a short space of time. Not a speckle of dust in sight!

The inspection had been done and I passed otherwise I would have been doing another round of cleaning. I had forgotten what it felt like being on my knees for such a long time! That was not the end of it as I was summoned to help with the cooking too. This part I didn't mind as I think it's hugely important to taste the mixture as you cook to ensure the flavours are blossoming flawlessly. That was my excuse! It worked, so why not?

The menu was mouth-watering indeed. There was chicken bhiryani, several curries, vegetarian and non-vegetarian options, and not to forget the starters - wholesome kebabs and spicy battered fish. No meal was complete without dessert and so ras malai was up for grabs. This desert would make any mouth dribble irrespective of if you have a sweet tooth or not. The delicious spongy oblong shaped sponge in a creamy milky sauce covered in different types of nuts delicious and cold. It was the Gucci of deserts. Right, enough of the food fantasies, time to get changed look pretty and wait for the clan to arrive.

CHAPTER 2

In came the herd, one by one. Each one was as loud as the other. Aunts, uncles, cousins, the whole lot of them. It was an extreme change of atmosphere from being so silent and mellow to a crazy fish market. However, it was so lovely to see them. Well, most of them. The non-stop chatter, the warm loving hugs were overdue and so needed. Time was flying and I didn't care if I was going to stay up all night catching up. Times like these were rare and I was going to make the most of every minute. I can honestly say I had never enjoyed washing up dishes so much. That was only because I had help and we were talking, joking and reminiscing all the way through. That night I was going to stay at my mum's whilst all the adults stayed at my grandmother's house. It was a tradition for us cousins to have a proper chill out and watch movies back to back with endless snacks. Let's face it you can't have one without the other. My disciplined diet had sure gone out of the window a long time ago!

I quickly packed a few essentials in my overnight bag. It didn't really matter if I had forgotten anything as I would only have to inconvenience myself of a short walk or better still a short drive. That would be very lazy of me, but hey I was on holiday. It was a nice feeling not to worry about my hair being in place or having to dress up in a certain way. I loved to scruff it up when I was not on shoots.

I felt so relaxed in my pyjamas and by this time everyone had settled in and was enjoying the quality time together. Unfortunately, as it was Christmas Eve we couldn't fulfil our normal ritual of going shopping to the supermarket for food at 3am and creating a harmless racket. Never the less we had the snow to keep us entertained. There was a thin layer of snow on the ground enough to have a snowball fight so why waste a golden opportunity? We put on our wellies, gloves scarves, hats and everything else that we could lay our hands on for the big fight! This is what I loved about my cousins as we all had an inner child that always came out to play when we got together. Smack! The first one hit me right in my eye.

This meant revenge so I rolled my tiny snowball in the snow till it became a healthy size then I had to line up my aim.

All lined up and there it went, bull's-eye right on my cousin's head who forgot to wear a hat. I was so proud of my victory that I decided to walk towards home and quit whilst I was ahead but then he came, my cousin, quicker than the speed of lightening and stuffed a hand load of snow down my back. Up north we call this tea-bagging! This went on for several hours into the night!

On Christmas morning, we all got up reluctantly and had breakfast courtesy of me. I didn't mind and so opted to make the easy option, bangers and mash which would keep us going nicely as we would be having a late lunch due to all the cooking that needed to be done as well as the fact that more of my cousins were coming from Manchester. I could not wait to see them it had been a ridiculously long time. My cousin from

Leicester mentioned that she had not long ago been away to Dubai. It was a family vacation and it wasn't the first time they had been there. They loved it because of the constant heat, how safe it was and more importantly that you could eat at any restaurant because it was halal. None of us eat non-halal food and so this seemed like a heavenly thought. I mean can you imagine walking into McDonald's and asking for a Big Mac? Such luxury!

The idea of walking in and ordering one of everything on the menu with meat in it made me very excited I must admit. It was sad but true! I was very intrigued and wanted to know more. She told me how beautiful Dubai was; exotic and rich in culture, easy to get around, and the people were really friendly. I was sold! This sounded like the heaven I needed. I wasn't even aware that the spoken language was Arabic up until that point. I certainly was learning more about the world. At that time in my life I was quite naïve, innocent and impressionable. I never went out to any of the after parties that I was invited to. I hated the whole networking thing. To me it was just full of toffee-nosed wannabes and attention seekers who want to be seen and heard. I am a northern lad and that's that. I was not going to pretend to be anything different.

The idea of being on a beach in the middle of winter was most appealing. The thought of going away was very comfortably planted in my head. Recommendations are most useful as at least I would know where to go what to do, where to eat. I carried on with my inquisition. Luckily my cousin was happy to oblige and by this time I had made up my mind for certain that I wanted to explore the delights of Dubai.

Back from the sunny delights of the mystic Middle East to the crippling cold in Accrington. What a crashing come down!

Time was seriously not on our side as it was time to head home and get the Christmas festivities on the way. One of my favourite films to watch over Christmas was 'A Christmas Carol', a film that I never get bored of. It had the same impact year in year out, a story with such a positive and powerful message! Due to the noise pollution, I didn't think being able to enjoy watching a film would be on the menu but turkey most certainly was!

There was a choice of a traditionally cooked turkey along with a spicy version. I had made up my mind that I would be trying both including all the trimmings, sprouts, carrots, gravy and so on.

One of my aunts from Leicester was a keen dessert maker and she brought over a variety of deserts each looking as gorgeous as the next. It would have been awfully rude not to try them all and without hesitation I did. My stomach had expanded to twice the size. I swore I would never eat a single thing for the rest of the year, as we all do.

All that anticipation for that one day and it was over before I knew it. Other than the mass amount of food that I had eaten, the thought of going away was strongly preying on my mind. The decision had been firmly made. I wanted to start the New

Year on a complete high by going away on New Year's Day, 2004.

There was so much to think about; packing, buying all the toiletries, booking tickets, finding a good hotel. The list was endless. Booking the ticket had to be my first mission and then I would have to work everything else around that. However, for that precise moment I wanted to enjoy quality time with my family then focus on my trip which seemed most surreal and hugely spontaneous and so close by.

Luckily it wasn't just me that was feeling sluggish. Everyone in the room felt the same way. That's Christmas for you at its best. Now the plans for Boxing Day! I always liked to hit the Boxing Day sales. It was one of my cheap thrills to get a bargain which I always did. I firmly believe that you do not have to pay lots of money to get a designer outfit. I wasn't going to accomplish this challenge on my own. I was going to drag anyone and everyone I could to come with me. The worst of it was that we would have to get up at 4am and leave for certain by 4.45am to get to Manchester city centre.

As you can imagine I didn't have many volunteers to come with me so it was time to use my powers of persuasion! Considering the situation, I did quite well as I managed to get my brother and one of my cousins to come with me.

The plan was to have a very early breakfast which I was more than happy to sort. I wouldn't want the troopers to be hungry.

We left around 5am all wrapped up nice and warm. The snow was minimal however the weather report said more snow was on its way.

I was wide awake and very chirpy surprisingly throughout the journey for that time of the morning. There were only a few cars on the road with the same sad intention of shopping such early hours no doubt. Parking was always a mission but on that particular day, I got a great slot just a ten-minute walk away from where all the excitement was about to take place. As we got out of the car about twenty yards down there was a very fashionable lady dressed up with her back to us. Tight fitting jeans, high heels, tailored coat the works. She looked hot and was no older than twenty-five. Little did we know that she was about to give us a shock and a jolt! She turned around and her face did not match the back view at all. It was like seeing two very different people. She had the face of an eighty-year-old woman. No teeth at the front except shining sparkling gums, saliva dribbling down her mouth making portable little puddles everywhere. Our mouths were touching the ground, luckily not near the saliva puddles!

The shock was intense. For once I was stuck for words but that was not all as this lady of the morning had some sweet words to share. She said in a very croaky northern accent whether we would like some business? Well put it this way we ran like crazy athletes until she was completely out of sight! Barely being able to breathe I burst into the biggest fits of laughter which spread along to my companions. We were giggling like school boys. I mean being propositioned at that time of the morning was quite a first! That had to be best wakeup call anyone has ever had!

As we were getting closer to the shopping mall on the high street the sound of hungry shoppers was becoming more evident. There were so many people ready to attack the shops like starved animals who were about to jump on their prey! Thankfully they had opened the doors of the mall which meant we would not freeze our backsides off outside. It was a case of queuing. We passed by a very popular shop where the queues were always at least a mile long. The queue looked like a huge snake wrapped around in swirls on the whole floor of the mall and then it happened, an argument broke out between two women. It got louder and louder to the point where actions were speaking louder than words. Both women looked so meek and mild and frail. Where did this aggression and strength come from? They went for it full pelt punches and all. One of them kept shouting 'I was here before you, stop pushing in you b***h!' Luckily, a lady with a pram managed to tear them apart and simmer things down.

It clearly was not an easy job. She struggled to make peace but succeeded eventually. I had to accept that it was going to be one of those days. Too much excitement in a short space of time!

I managed to plough through my list of things that I had to buy and made it out of the mall alive. I needed mainly summer clothing as it was going to be quite hot in Dubai. The rest of the things like sun block etc I could leave till the next day and get it locally.

The realisation of what I was doing kicked in more and more. It was really happening! I was going to Dubai, whoohoo! I managed to retain my excitement on the outside even though I wanted to scream in delight. I still hadn't told anyone officially that I was going away. I thought it best to break the news sooner rather than later as I didn't want to leave my grandparents in the lurch. They had regular doctors and hospital appointments. I would need to make arrangements with someone to ensure that they didn't miss any of their appointments.

I wanted to book my ticket in the evening. I just needed a reasonably priced ticket. I was totally in the mind set of going and so it had to happen.

After a productive morning of shopping and glamorous entertainment, the guilt of dragging my brother and cousin in the cold with me melted away as we all ended up buying something and no so one came back empty handed thankfully. It was time to go home and relax and enjoy the rest of the day with family as everyone would be heading back home late that evening.

Timed perfectly well, we all strolled in with our bags whilst the table was being laid for lunch which meant I got out of table duties. Lunch seemed very rushed and after demolishing the Christmas leftovers my cousins and everyone got their bags together ready to head home. We said our goodbyes but in our true traditional style it was an hour later that people actually left the house. Why break a habit of a lifetime?

The silence was hugely evident. I always felt sad when people left. I am a very sensitive person and hate saying goodbyes. There was a great solution to end the sadness and that was to go to my sister's house and hang out there and spend some quality time with my nephew who was only four years old then. He really is my world. The cutest kid with such a cool personality, just like his uncle of course! I could also do some research on the internet and book my ticket.

At that time, I didn't have a laptop or computer so it was either going to my sister's house to use her PC or the local library where they knew me by my first name as I practically lived there. My information technology skills were far from good but thanks to the head librarian I managed to develop my skills much more quickly and smoothly. Smart phones were non-existent so it wasn't possible to send emails at my convenience.

It's all about the food in an Asian household just in case you hadn't clocked on. My sister insisted we eat and I didn't hesitate at all. After dinner, I decided to have a little hunt round online to see what bargain I could bag. It really was a case of having high tolerance levels and lots of patience. As I was scrolling down, to my misery the prices of tickets to Dubai were ridiculously high. We were talking £700 which was way beyond my budget. I set my budget at £400 and refused to pay a penny more.

I came across the teletext page which supposedly had the best deals going. They were even willing to price match. This seemed more promising. I must have flicked through what seemed like thousands of pages and my patience was wearing really thin then my eye caught sight of big bold red letters on the screen saying 'final sale', a further 20% off if I booked there and then. I had to click on a different page to see the deal. As I clicked on the screen there was an interruption with the internet connection. I could have cried I had got so close. As if by some miraculous recovery the page came back about five minutes later and there it was Dubai via Istanbul for £360 with Turkish airways. I couldn't believe my luck. A cheap ticket under my budget! A job well done however the mission wasn't fully complete as I needed to ensure that the dates would tally up with when I wanted to leave and return.

So, sifting through, reading every bit of the small print I put in the date of departure which was 31st December 2003 returning on the 15th January 2004. A good two weeks would be ample for me to re-energise and feel completely normal again. The connection was so slow which was causing me anxiety. Finally, there it was in clear black and white on the screen, the availability of the flight I wanted. I quickly got my card from my wallet and did the deeds. All booked! No going back now. It all happened so quickly. The reality of the situation dawned on me and I must admit I became a bit nervous. I had never had a connecting flight before. How did it all work? Will it be clearly sign posted at the airport? These thoughts were all rummaging in my head. I managed to calm down eventually. The bottom line was that I was going away from the cold to the heat!

As I was travelling alone and going to a place totally alien to me, a friend of mine suggested I should check out a website called www.expatriates.com to get a good insight of what there is to do in Dubai. I would be connecting with other British people who lived there and with people who have travelled to Dubai who would be sharing their thoughts and honest views. That was the next task. I signed up. It was an easy process and very straight forward. It was very interesting to read the comments on the forum that people had written.

Generally, people were saying how amazing Dubai was and that there was always something to do there and that I would never want to leave once I got there. I felt a streak of excitement run through my body. I am the kind of person that loves to connect with people from all over the world. This was a prime opportunity to make some friends online and so I decided to leave a message on the forum saying, 'Hi, how are you all? I am Nadeem and I will be in Dubai on the 1st January. I would really like to hear from anyone who has any recommendations of what area is the best place to be based in whilst in Dubai and any specific tours I should book. Look forward to hearing from you, Nadeem.'

That was it. I was so hoping that someone would read my message. If no one did then I would find my own way around which was thrilling to some degree but some guidance would be much more helpful. I tried to remember some of the places my cousin mentioned. The one that particularly came to mind was Jumeirah. I did a quick search online and looked at a map of the United Arab Emirates. Dubai is just one part of the

Emirates as there are seven parts to the Emirates which makes up the United Arab Emirates. The others are Sharjah, Abu Dhabi, Ajman, Fujeira, Ras Al Khaimah and Umm Suqeim. I saw that Jumeirah seemed a bit out from the central point of Dubai.

Ideally, I wanted to be more centrally located so that it would be easier to manoeuvre around. Whilst doing my research I was curious to know what currency is used there and what the going rate was against the British pound. The currency used in Dubai is Dirhams and at that time it was roughly five Dirhams to the pound. Not too bad by the sounds of it as apparently food and transport was cheap so I was told. The main forms of getting around would be by bus or taxi. No trains at all, then. According to the map Dubai looked quite small so surely the distance from one end to the other wouldn't be too much of a trek?

In all the excitement, I had forgotten the fact that I needed somewhere to sleep too.

Tiredness was really kicking in and so I decided that I would look at hotels the following day. I turned off the computer and went back to the living room to join the others. There was something that I needed to do. What was it? I was picking my brains trying to remember and then eventually the penny dropped. I had to tell everyone that I was going on holiday literally in a few days! *'Guys I'm off, see ya later'*. Well, maybe not quite in that manner. I strolled into the living room with a huge grin. I tried to control myself but I just couldn't. I went into the direction of my nephew and started playing with him. My paternal side was in full swing. By this time my mum had come and joined our little gathering. It came out without any control, 'I am going to Dubai on Wednesday'. I could not believe how it just came out! The reaction of the faces in front of me said it all. The reaction was not a bad one just a mild shocked one. I explained that I had been feeling extremely exhausted and over-worked and that I seriously needed some time out to regain my sanity. The real selling point was my cousin saying how amazing Dubai was and how much of a learning trip this would be for me. Everyone was very happy for me. Great, I got the thumbs up!

My mind still felt so clogged up. I had and still have the memory of a goldfish, I just don't remember anything unless I write it down so I started to make a list of things I needed. Luckily, I had annual travel insurance which was one less thing to worry about. I must admit I was good at keeping my travel bags compact. Having practically living out of a suitcase for work, I became a master at getting everything into the suitcase without having to sit on it to close it. I don't know why I was worrying so much as I had plenty of time. The following day was going to be another shopping day, hopefully not a stressful one. The night ended on a real high with great conversations and putting the world to rights. Another day closer to my adventure! Bring it on!

A lie in was desperately needed. The last few days had been hectic, lots of late nights with a maximum three or four hours sleep here and there. It was all building up. It must have been around 1pm that I casually got out of bed. I decided to have a light lunch, some tea and toast. I couldn't be bothered to cook a gourmet meal even though I was very passionate about cooking. Time was ticking along and I had a lot to do before Wednesday. The good thing was my flight was an overnight flight which meant I still had the whole day of Wednesday to relax and panic about last minute things that needed doing.

It was quite a fresh and crisp afternoon, perfect to take a nice stroll into Accrington town centre. It wasn't really a backwater; after all we had a Marks & Spencer's, the very branch where I had my stint in retail over a Christmas period. I must have been the youngest person there and the second Asian person. The other staff members were born there and devout workers, all fifty years old plus of course. Most of them were miserable as hell with a just a minority who were friendly and normal. My days there were numbered. I knew it! The last straw was being told off for clock watching. It was a beautiful clock and the only bit of excitement there!

Shortly after, I decided to say my goodbyes to the only few members of staff that I considered to be normal! The best thing was that a few months after I left there I got a modelling job for Marks & Spencer's. My picture was in all the stores on the walls. What a mark to leave! This gave me a feeling of sheer satisfaction. There was no getting away from me!

The plan of action was to run into the one shop that housed everything I needed and get out. That's exactly what I did. Another mission complete! The next chore was to go home and start the packing. I also needed to check my emails to make sure the airline had emailed me all the relevant details. I had decided to pack my portfolios too. I don't know what possessed me to want to take them but my babies were coming with me too. In terms of material things apart from my mobile phone my portfolios were my second most prised possessions.

I love the whole routine of travelling from packing your bags to getting to the airport and reaching your destination. It's equally thrilling every time.

Panic over, the travel agent had sent my travel tickets and confirmation. To my surprise I had also received notifications to say that I had received some messages on the expatriate's website. I was very curious indeed to read them and see who had responded. I had about five messages from the same person. Someone called Ethan who was living in Dubai. Originally from Sao Paolo, Brazil, Ethan worked in one of the most opulent hotels based in Dubai. He seemed very friendly and helpful which was a great start. He was kind enough to say that he would look into booking a hotel for me that wouldn't cost too much and that he would be really happy to meet me at the airport on the day of my arrival. I was so touched by these kind gestures. I mean who has the time to do this in this day and age? There were a lot of messages back and forth which were very assuring. He suggested we swap numbers just in case anything happened and we couldn't find each other at the airport. It was a great idea, so that's exactly what I did. This was another huge peace of mind for me. Everything was falling into place seamlessly.

I couldn't believe I was actually flying out in just a matter of hours. It came so quickly. Everything was done and dusted.

Being an organised person does help lower the stress levels however there is always something to stress about if you are a born worrier like me; a typical Scorpio! My suitcase was quite big in size but manageable to cart around. I had one hand luggage bag too which had my tickets, passport, money and my model portfolios.

An early night was a must. I wanted to see everyone before I went. I don't know why but I had a gut feeling that I should say goodbye to everyone before leaving the country. It really was a strange feeling. Naturally I didn't think too much into it and so off I went to dreamland smiling like a Cheshire cat!

CHAPTER 3

I must have slept for a good eight hours which was a lot for me. I was feeling very refreshed and very ready for my trip. The sun was shining. What a beautiful day it was despite the cold that was coming through from the open windows. I showered and got dressed. I wanted to be comfortable, yet trendy. My hair took less time than normal to style. I didn't feel hungry at all and so decided to skip breakfast. I took my luggage downstairs to the hallway. Unfortunately, no one was able to take me to the airport due to other commitments which wasn't a problem. I was more than happy to jump on the train. The only annoying thing was that I would have to change trains. No biggie. I called up everyone that I wanted to see before leaving. They all came soon after to wish me well on my quest to discover the mystique of the Middle East.

Thankfully I had managed to arrange for someone to take my grandparents to their appointments too. I always worried a lot about them. They were getting old and frail but they always remained so jovial and so loving regardless. My grandfather was a huge inspiration to me. A very strong person that had seen and experienced so much in life! When I was very young, roughly about two or three years of age I suffered from epileptic fits. On this one occasion, I stopped breathing. I was turning blue and everyone went into panic mode but it was my grandfather that composed himself and gave me mouth to mouth resuscitation and brought me round again. He saved my life!

My aunt Afshan, who I am very close to, gave me a lift to the railway station. She was only a few years older than me, always on good form and great company. We had always got on from a very early age and had the relationship of a brother and sister rather than aunt and nephew. After school we used to go to Quranic lessons together, along with another aunt of mine. Wonderful memories! It must have taken a whole three minutes to get to the railway station. We said our goodbyes and that was it, me, myself and I. For once the train was running on time. To be fair the journey was only going to be about forty-five minutes. I got on with my case and managed to find some space for it. It wasn't very busy on the train. I could finally switch off for a bit and try and absorb the fact that I was going away.

I reached Manchester Airport bang on time. By this time, I was starving and needed some food. I always loved travelling from Manchester as the airport is so beautifully designed, so sleek, modern and airy. I thought it best to check my bag in first then search for food.

The lady at the desk was very friendly and approachable. The whole transaction was very smooth and hassle free. I was in the mood for a sandwich and chips. A weird combination, but a great one undoubtedly! The chips were dripping in ketchup and mayonnaise, just the way I liked it. I knocked down the food within no time; I was stuffed to the core. I needed to keep reminding myself that I was going via Istanbul otherwise I would be sitting at the wrong gate and miss my flight. I had never been to Istanbul. It seemed a very intriguing place. I had a weakness for history and learning about different cultures. It really got me going, and still does! The stop-over in Istanbul was only a short one which was great. There was nothing worse than having a long stop over and being stuck within the walls of the airport.

Four hours to Istanbul then a few more hours to Dubai and that was it. I would be reaching Dubai 7.30am Dubai time. Even though Ethan had assured me he would meet me at the other end, there were no guarantees as I barely knew him. I just wanted to enjoy my journey and chill rather than clutter my head with more stress. That was the whole purpose of getting away.

I comfortably got to Istanbul without any hassles or complications. It was a great flight. I was lucky enough not to have had anyone sitting next to me. The next part was going to be a bit tricky. I needed to know where to go to get my connecting flight. I got off the plane and tried to find signs that would direct me to the gate number for my next flight. To be honest I didn't know what signs I needed to look out for. I was going by my instincts and started following a mass of people who looked like they knew where they were going. I was waiting in the queue looking like a lost puppy. It was my turn to show my passport to the man at the desk. I showed him my passport and he said that I had come to the wrong end; I had crossed the line which meant I was technically in Istanbul and that I needed to pay for a visa. This was all gobbledygook to me.   I mean how can crossing a line make such a huge difference? It wasn't making any sense. Still none the wiser I paid for the visa to keep the peace which cost around £10, the man stamped my passport and I was on my way to where I should be. It seemed so complicated or was it me? After doing a whole circuit of the airport I finally came to the gate where it clearly stated that the flight from that gate was going to Dubai. I was not going to move at any cost!

It was nice to feel relaxed and carefree. However, that was short lived as boarding time had approached but there was no one to be seen. No staff no passengers, no one! It was time to panic. There had been no announcements made or any information given.

What was going on? I was too agitated to wait so decided to go and ask someone. Trying to find a member of staff wasn't the easiest of tasks either. Eventually I managed to corner a member of staff and they said the gate number had changed and that if I didn't run fast to the correct gate I would miss my flight. I couldn't believe my luck. I would have gone to the right gate had they been bothered enough to communicate with everyone. I ran for my life and just about made it to the gate as it was closing. I smiled my best smile with my pearly whites all out on display. It worked! Hooray!

I always preferred to be seated by a window, which I had thankfully. It felt like the only form of contact with the outside world when being up thousands of feet. In my row of seats which was in the middle section of the plane, all the seats were occupied. It would have been nice if I had an empty seat next to me for some personal space. I got to my seat and put my hand luggage in the compartment above. There was another passenger a good healthy twenty stone man sat in the middle seat. I squeezed past him with great difficulty and fell into my seat. I tried to get as comfortable as I could, but no such joy.

Finally, up in the air and all seemed calm. Dinner was to be served soon after. I didn't really mind what was given as long as it was reasonably edible. I wasn't in a position to be fussy. There came the trolley dolly, as old as my grandmother, bless her. She couldn't even spare a smile to expose her shiny gums. She literally threw the food at me, *what a silly and unprofessional cow*, which was running through my head. I managed to salvage most of which was lying on my lap but I didn't dare to challenge her as she would have happily eaten me alive and not even spat me out!

It wasn't a great dinner, just a messy shepherd's pie with a few boring vegetables along with a miniscule piece of cake that tasted like it had lived many centuries. It was hard enough to be used as a cricket ball. I guess it was better than starving.

I was in desperate of a nap. I wanted to feel fresh for when I landed in Dubai, and enjoy every second of my trip. This was another challenge within itself as my friend next to me was snoring away and had somehow managed to get even closer to me to the point where the only way I could have a bit of comfort was to shove my face in the tiny window. By this time, I was really losing patience. *Calm down*, I thought to myself. It wasn't worth the stress. Trying to think happy thoughts, eventually I managed to get a bit of sleep. When I awoke my neighbour was still asleep. I had to give him a powerful nudge.

He got up looking quite embarrassed as half of his body was on me. He slowly moved over to his own side enabling me to breathe more easily. It was about 7.15am and we were descending.

The views from above were quite spectacular as all you could see was the desert sand, a very rich golden colour. The excitement was beginning to build up more and more. The landing was bump free too! I always enjoyed hearing the senior crew member welcoming everyone to the country of arrival both in English and native language.

I was officially in Dubai! I had to wait quite a while as my friend, to whom I had still not uttered a single word, was in no hurry to leave. We must have been the last passengers off the plane. As I came down the aircraft stairs, I was hit with the heat, a good twenty-three degrees at that time of the morning? I took a deep breath and fully embraced it because I loved the heat. I entered the airport and was so taken back by the décor which was so tastefully done. Nice bright colours, not too over the top. They had what looked like palm trees inside the airport with golden fairy lights on them. The thing that hit me the most was the fact it was so clean. Not even a speckle of dust was in sight. This built up a great impression of the UAE before I had even stepped outside.

I got straight through immigration without any problems for a change. Normally I would always get stopped regardless of where I was and grilled with lots of random questions, was it the face or name, who knows? I grabbed my suitcase still admiring all that my eyes were seeing. For a short while I had totally forgotten that Ethan would be meeting me on the other side. I must admit I did begin to feel nervous. Worst case scenario: if he turned out to be a weirdo, I could always make an excuse and do my own thing!

As I exited the airport, there was a white plaque in front of me with my name written on it in clear big bold letters and holding the plaque was a tall slender built guy with scraped back sleek and shiny hair. The hair was so tightly pulled back that not even a single loose strand could be seen or escape for that matter. He was dressed in white linen trousers and a loose white linen shirt. He knew immediately that I was the one he was waiting for. I headed in his direction and he shook my hand and hugged me. The formalities were out of the way, he seemed like a nice chilled out guy who had a lot to say. He said he found a cheap hotel in an area called Deira which is very central.

I was beginning to feel much more relaxed in general, couldn't believe that I was finally in Dubai. Ethan and I got along very well; it was like we had known each other for a long time. I have that kind of personality where if I think you are nice and genuine, and giving me your time, I will go out of my way for you no matter what, that is just the way I am. This was surely blossoming into a great friendship.

He reconfirmed that he worked in a luxury hotel. To be honest to this day I have no idea what his job role was. The plan was that he was to drop me off to my hotel and then he would head home and do what he needed to. I could freshen up and then we would meet in the evening. We got a taxi quite easily, to my surprise. The taxis are well maintained with air conditioning and are also government owned which means no haggling on price as they go by the meter. The taxi driver put my luggage into the boot of the car very neatly and we were ready to go. I was truly amazed by the buildings that I could see out of the window. Each one outdoing the other! From what I could see, Dubai was a very sleek and modern place. I didn't have any expectations but I was more than satisfied. The flow of the conversation was in full swing and before I knew it we had arrived at the destination that was going to be my home for a while. It really felt like I was in the hub of the city which excited me. It's a great way to get to know the locals and fit in. Ethan was kind enough to escort me to my room taking my suitcase. A service I sure could get used to!

Even though I was only going to be in Dubai for a short time, Ethan suggested that the best and cheapest way to keep in touch would be is to buy a local SIM card which was a great idea. As it was New Year's Day, that would take me a few days to sort out. It felt very much like I was away on holiday as I was in the heat, normally I would be in England in the freezing cold. It was so different here in Dubai, yet so nice and welcoming.

The hotel room wasn't that big in size. It had a window with a great view. It was definitely a budget hotel working out to be about the equivalent of £45 per night. To be honest, how much time was I going to spend inside? I wanted to see as much as I could while I was here, and experience everything and say that I covered the whole of Dubai. The tiredness was kicking in now but I was way too curious about the area I was staying in so I decided to take a little stroll. It wasn't very busy due to the siesta they have in Dubai from about 1pm to 4.30pm. I had read this online whilst doing some research. It was seriously quiet. I did a good circuit then headed back to the hotel where I flung myself on the bed. I was really tired so I needed to make sure that I set the alarm otherwise I would be sleeping through to the next day. I set the alarm for about 5pm which would give me enough time to get ready. I was out like a light!

I was woken up with the horrific sound of my alarm on my phone. I intentionally have it set on a horrific tune because then it is guaranteed to annoy me enough to get me out of bed. I had a nice shower and got dressed into what we call in the modelling world smart casuals; just a pair of navy linen trousers and a white t-shirt. Nice simple look for the evening. I had barely been there and I could already see the change in my skin tone.

I was all ready for about 6.30pm and still had about an hour to kill so I decided to go for another walk. The heat was quite intense. The atmosphere was so different. It was so lively and buzzing with lots of people in the streets as the shops were now open. I could predominantly hear people speak Urdu and Hindi which I speak fluently. This was so unexpected! At least I would be able to haggle at the bazaars and get around more comfortably. I was an amazing haggler if there ever was one. I always got the price I initiated. I must have been wandering around for a good forty minutes before deciding to head back and wait in the lobby of the hotel as Ethan would be there soon.

I got myself well acquainted with the receptionist who was very curious to know where I was from. He was convinced I was Arab. He himself was from Kerala in India. I had noticed whilst walking around that there seemed to be a big Indian and Pakistani community in Dubai. Kam, the receptionist explained that a lot of people came to Dubai from south Asia to work as the work prospects were much better abroad. It all began to make more sense now.

Ethan arrived with his hair exactly in the same place as before and we headed out. My first night out in Dubai! It was a very exciting feeling!

He said we would go to a restaurant in Al Rigga an area not too far from me to a restaurant called 'Beirut'. Apparently, they did the best shawarma which is basically either a meat or chicken wrap accompanied with a selection of pickled vegetables. It's a typical Arabic dish. My mouth was watering at the thought. I was starving!

We were walking amidst all the activity in the streets from market traders to fresh juice sellers, all wanting to lure us in. It seemed to be getting busier and busier but for me the crowds just added more charm to the place.

The conversation turned towards me and why I ended up in Dubai. I said that I was highly recommended by family. He said I made the right choice and that I would fall in love with Dubai the more I saw of it.

The restaurant was definitely a great choice, buzzing with very well-groomed people. This was my kind of place!

The men were so suave and polished; their beards shaped so precisely, hair coiffed to perfection, and the long white robe also known as a dishdash giving them an angelic look. The ladies were all in black from head to toe. Some wore the niqab, or face veil, revealing the most hypnotic eyes painted to perfection, while others wore an elegantly wrapped hijab, or head scarf.

They would glide so flawlessly with their designer high heels and no doubt designer attire underneath the abaya (long black robe for women.) You could smell the money!

It was beginning to sound like a fish market now and my stomach was doing somersaults due to hunger. As it was New Year's Day it was busier than normal which meant our orders would take longer to get to us. The restaurant was not fancy but very inviting. A full restaurant is always a sign of a good restaurant according to me. Ethan was more than happy for the short wait as he smoked like a chimney and so needed his fix. I personally hate the smell of cigarettes. I hate how it seeps into your hair and body. It's a vile smell and habit as far as I am concerned. A cosy little table right beside the window became available and I dived to get it. The waiter came and started to speak in Arabic with me but I didn't understand what he was saying apart from a couple of words which are the same in Urdu. Again, he thought I was Arab. He spoke broken English as did most of the people. All I could think of was that shawarma. I went for a meat and chicken mix wrap with fries, salad and pickles. I ripped into it like I had never seen food before. Ethan went for the same dish. It was delicious. The meat just melted in my mouth. I had smothered chilli sauce on my fries as always. Surely it tasted that much more amazing because of my hunger.

'So, you are a model' Ethan said in quite a weird tone as if to insinuate that the type of modelling I did was more of the adult nature. I cut through and said, 'yes a fashion and commercial model', before any other insinuations were made. The usual questions came up; *how did you start, what kind of work have you done* etc. He then said modelling was something that he had wanted to do for a long time but the opportunity hadn't come up and that maybe I could help him launch his career. He was a very confident person, maybe a bit *too* confident as he commented that he would be a very sought-after model and that he would become very famous very quickly because of his amazingly good looks. I was here on vacation, not here to sort people's careers! It was too much too soon! I told him how I had also completed presentation assignments for television and radio. He seemed quite intrigued but for his own purpose only. This was beginning to wind me up I must admit.

He then salvaged himself by saying that I should meet one of his very good friends, Luca Hadad who worked in media in Dubai and who would be very interested to meet me because of my media background.

I loved meeting people from all walks of life. I found that you could learn so much from each other in so many ways.

The night was drawing to a close as Ethan needed to get home because he was working early the next couple of days which meant I would be venturing out on my own. We would be in contact to arrange our next meet up. He got a taxi back home whilst I was too busy still feeling the buzz of being away and so decided to wonder the streets of Dubai aimlessly.

CHAPTER 4

Having had a bit of a restless night of tossing and turning I got up feeling quite tired. I needed some caffeine to bring me round. Yesterday on the way back I had noticed a little café that served Indian tea which is rich, creamy sweet and full of happiness. I could see the humongous tea pots with the tea being brewed which will have been going for many hours as that's the secret that gives it that unique taste. I quickly showered and got dressed to get my cuppa. It was such a cute little place with so much character on my doorstep. I went inside and was served immediately. Coffee or tea? Tough decision as I was having fantasies about tea. The guy behind the counter recommended the coffee. Always up for trying something different! It was served to me in what looked like a shot glass. It was hotter than hot! I just about managed to put it down in time before burning my hand. They had a million cans of rainbow stacked up everywhere. I was intrigued by what this was and the gentleman explained that it was evaporated milk and it was used religiously in tea and coffee to give it that extra kick. I must admit that coffee tasted very special. I decided that I would be getting my teas and coffees from there every morning.

It was another scorcher of a day. Before heading out I needed to text my sister as forgot to do it the day before with the excitement of being in Dubai, just to let her know that I got here safely. She would then let my mum and everyone else know. The last thing I needed was for everyone to start panicking about my wellbeing whilst I was busy enjoying myself with not a care in the world. I always like to be spontaneous so I didn't set myself a rigid schedule. I went back to my room just to apply sun block and get my sunglasses. Another thing I did notice was that there were no dodgy looking insects in sight. I had brought my insect repellent just in case. For now, the coast was clear. I have very sweet blood and anything and everything does normally enjoy a good chomp on me.

I asked the receptionist for recommendations of where I could go today. He mentioned that a bit further down from the hotel, just a ten-minute walk, they had boats going to old Dubai known as Bur Dubai. He said it was very cheap to hop on and off and that they were regular. That was very appealing, so yes let's give it a go. He also mentioned about Nasser square, also known as Banyas Square where I could find restaurants and a water fountain still in Deira. It was all just a walk away. I love walking so off I went heading towards Nasser square first. He was absolutely right, just a few minutes later I was there right in front of this beautiful fountain. As I looked to the right of me I saw KFC, and opposite was Mcdonald's.

I was squealing in delight. Sad, I know. It just meant I could I could eat anything off the menu as it was halal. I walked around the fountain enjoying the cool splashes of water then sat down on an empty bench. It was such a special feeling to sit down and absorb the views. I felt very relaxed and so de-stressed. Such a serene moment! As I hadn't had any breakfast apart from my very special coffee, it was time I did it! Yes, I would go to Mcdonald's and have my very first Big Mac. I was going all the way, a large portion of fries with that slightly sweet curry sauce and a strawberry milkshake. I was seriously living life on the edge. It was exactly like any other branch. I placed my order and was beaming with excitement. Lord behold, there before my very eyes was my Big Mac. I took a bite with such anticipation but to be honest it wasn't all that, simply a burger in a bun with lettuce and mayonnaise sauce. What a let-down. It was so bland in taste too. I hadn't been missing anything all these years after all! I still ate it as I hate wasting food. The milkshake however was so fulfilling so creamy and fruity and most certainly compensated for the lack of flavours in the burger.

So back to my travels! It was time to see what this boat area was about. It was such an easy route, just straight ahead and there the boats were, all parked up on the other side. I used the subway to get across and it was sparkling with cleanliness. I got onto the boat with a host of strangers. It soon filled up with bodies and away we went. We were to hand over just one Dirham to the driver which is equivalent to about twenty-five pence. I mean how cheap is that? Not only was it cheap but it was a beautiful way of travelling to get to the other side. The views were simply spectacular. There was a warm breeze. I was in my element. I could do this every day. It was only a very short journey but a pleasant one. As I stepped off the boat it was like stepping back in time. The bazaars or markets were very traditional looking and authentic. I walked around as the stall

43

sellers would try their utmost to sell me anything they could, from clothes, to ornaments, nuts, shisha pipes and genuine silver jewellery. The smells of the spices were so seductive and enticing. It was like Aladdin's cave.

Being very much into fashion I spotted a couple of tailors. There was one particular shop called White Eagle Tailors that seemed very keen to gain my custom. I went inside and the first thing they asked was, 'what would you like to drink?' What great customer service. Even if you had no intention of buying anything you would be thinking about it now. I really fancied some tea and within no time at all it arrived, piping hot and delicious. I fell into their trap and decided to get a pair of trousers made. They took all my measurements and gave me the most reasonable price.

A win-win situation! It didn't end there as they said they it would only take two days to make. I was overwhelmed with the speed of completion.

I carried on walking and passed the Dubai museum which looked very inviting. I had plenty of time and so could tick that off another day. Opposite the museum was Meena Bazaar, an area full of Indian clothing, jewellery shops and Indian restaurants. Mini Mumbai! This was so different to what I expected which I really loved. It was a real eclectic mix which was what I loved about this city. It catered for everyone. It was nice just being on my own. I loved being with people but I loved my own company too. I felt so glad that I had come. I headed back towards the boats, (*shakhtura* in Arabic), to enjoy the mesmerising views all for one Dirham. As I was lost in this amazingness, the most unusual thought crossed my mind. I had only been there for two days and I wanted to live there. I never got homesick and I always wanted to live wherever I travelled but this time it just felt so unusually different. This feeling was so strong and weird. I couldn't explain it. One part of my mind was having an intense discussion with the other side about this. What was going on? My attention was diverted by the boat rocking from side to side as people were getting off and one side of the boat held more weight. I was feeling a little tired and so decided to have a power nap at the hotel before going to a mall later for a spot of shopping and dinner. Tonight, I was going to be more adventures with my food.

I bagged a cab literally outside the hotel. It was so nice and clean from inside. I got chatting with the driver, as you do, and he was telling me that he was from Pakistan. He had been living here for about three years. All his family were based in Pakistan including his wife and children. He hadn't seen them for about two years. Now that's sad. Can you imagine missing out so much time on your child growing up? Not that I have children but having a nephew was close enough. He explained that where he was from, the job opportunities were few and far between. He had a friend who came to Dubai and was doing reasonably well and that was how he came to live here. The conversation was in Urdu which is why I think he opened up so much.

Here I stood in this swanky looking mall. It was clean enough to eat your dinner off the floor and that's no joke. The most disappointing thing for me as I was browsing around was the fact that that they had so many high street names that were easily accessible in England. I came here for some culture and instead I got M&S, Next, and so on, the list just went on. The only western shop that put a smile on my face was Virgin Music.

I love my music, especially Arabic music as it has such a provocative dance beat that makes you want to bust some moves, regardless of where you are! This was a golden opportunity to stock up on my collection.

There was only so much time you could spend in a mall. No more shopping. It was time to fill a hole. The food court was surprisingly very varied with so much choice. As I panned round my eye caught the bright red lights of a sign for Chinese cuisine. Decision made, dinner sorted.

As I headed towards the taxi stand that strange thought popped up into my head again, the one about moving here. How serious was I about this? What would I do for work? Where would I live? How realistically could I do this? I knew that I only had one shot at life; I couldn't live in regret. It was important to go with my heart and just do it! The idea of living in the heat with such a picturesque backdrop was more than just appealing. *Why not give it a go, see where it lands you*, I thought to myself, as my face cracked with a big smile. The best thing to do was to have a basic plan then build on it and work towards it. I had always dreamt of living abroad. Maybe this was a sign flashing in front of my very eyes. I couldn't just ignore it. Everything happened for a reason. I remembered what Ethan had said previously about a friend that worked in media over here. I could ask him for guidance. His company may even be interested in hiring me. There was a blatant opportunity here and I needed to grab it with both hands. So, first things first, I had to try and set up this meeting with Ethan's friend as soon as possible to get the ball rolling. I didn't want to come across as desperate. I needed to play it very cool.

As soon as I got home I text messaged Ethan to ask him when we would be meeting up. He said the following day. He also mentioned that he would bring his friend Luca too. Fantastic! I didn't need to say anything. It all pulled together itself without much effort. I was a very happy boy!

I really needed a local SIM card as I was dreading thinking what my mobile bill would be when I went back home, that's if I was going back. All these ifs about going back made the whole situation seem very surreal. The days seemed to be running ahead of me. I was finding it difficult to keep up. Even though I had only been here for such a short while I was bonding with it at an incredible speed. It just seemed a natural progression.

All ready for another day. I got my coffee fix from my local and headed towards the office of Etisalat the main network provider for mobiles at that time. Apparently, all I needed was my passport to be able to get a SIM card. I got there and it was flooded with people. It was in numerical order.

I got my ticket and managed to find a seat. An hour had passed then two, then three. This was getting ridiculous. I reminded myself that I didn't have a crazy schedule to adhere by so it was fine to wait patiently. Finally, it was my turn. The representative didn't look like a happy chappy so I tried to make conversation to break the ice. I wasn't getting anywhere. I showed him all he needed to see then he thrust a form in front of me, talk about customer services! I quickly filled it out almost scared as he wasn't the happiest person around. Then he put a selection of SIM cards on the table and gave me a choice of numbers. I grabbed the nearest one to me, so that I could be out in a flash. He took my phone and kindly put the SIM card into it, then explained the procedure of when it would become active. Finally the moment I had been waiting for happened, he cracked a small smile, thanked me and let me be on my way. Result!

I really wanted to speak to my grandmother and mum so I gave them a quick bell. They were so happy to hear my voice. Clearly, they were missing me. How would they feel if I moved away? Time would tell for sure. I also called Ethan to confirm the plans for that evening. Just to keep things less complicated we decided to meet back at Beirut restaurant.

I really loved the sweet warm evenings. By walking the majority of the time, I had got quite confident with my directions. I was wearing a thin black shirt and a pair of slim fitting jeans. My hair was a bit wilder than normal but why not? It was important to make a good impression. As I walked past some of the perfumeries I was hit with a concoction of different Arabic smells. Strong enough to seduce anyone! Smelling nice was always so important to me. I enjoyed bathing myself in colognes and leaving a trail. The atmosphere was in its full glory. People seemed so content unlike some of the miserable faces you saw on the streets back home. Surely that was a good enough reason to relocate to another country? I was getting very comfortable and I refused to fight it.

Just a few yards away, I was looking forward to seeing the guys. Ethan spotted me and got up to greet me. Sat beside him was a reasonably tall guy wearing a beige blazer, jeans and a smart shirt. Very fair skinned with green eyes. As Ethan greeted me he introduced his friend Luca who at this point was standing up too. We shook hands and sat down in our seats. Luca seemed a very jovial fun person. He was chatting away and was interested in what I was saying. It was a very nice relaxed atmosphere. We ordered some fresh juices and then got back into our conversations. I learnt that Luca was not from Dubai but Lebanon. He didn't have a typical Gulf look so I assumed he was not a local. He was telling me that he worked for a big media company called 'Al Fursan' and that he was quite high up in his post.

The company he worked for apparently produced lifestyle programmes for the UAE. I got goose bumps when he mentioned this. How amazing would that be to have a great job in media and live in Dubai. It would certainly be living the high life as in Dubai British citizens are very much looked up to, and looked after too which means salaries offered are of a very healthy sum he said. In some cases, they give accommodation too. My eyes were lighting up. Ethan had briefly briefed him on my media background. He was intrigued to know more. I told him as well as modelling I am a presenter and that I did my media training with the BBC and so on. He was extremely impressed. He said I had a lot of credentials behind me, a great personality and that I was a very interesting person, would I every consider working in Dubai. At this point I almost choked on my drink. I very calmly responded with the fact that I had been having an amazing time discovering Dubai and that I had bonded with it hugely.

I don't know how I managed to keep myself so composed. Everything I had wished for was coming true so seamlessly. He said that if I didn't mind he would like to talk to his seniors about me as I would be a great asset to the company and with my wealth of experience I could have a thriving career in Dubai. This was truly unbelievable. I did not think for a second how quickly things could develop overnight.

Ethan seemed a bit quiet this evening. Occasionally I would catch him looking at me from the corner of my eye in quite a discomforting way. I just felt really uneasy. Then as if by a switch of a button he became normal again. Maybe he was overworked? It's good to give people benefit of the doubt. That's the way I always thought. We ordered a mezze which basically is a platter with everything on it from meat to cheese, dips the whole works. It was quite substantial amount as they provided some fresh baked bread to go with it. As I was feeling so happy and on top of the world with my new venture I decided to announce that I would give it a go and stay in Dubai. I was not going back to England and that was final. What a decision to make so quickly. It was quite different to deciding what colour of shoes to buy. I liked to live for the moment and was not going to miss out on an opportunity of a lifetime. The boys seemed quite excited too. However, Luca seemed more content out of the two to be honest. We raised a toast to me and my new beginnings. I was still in shock. What a surreal moment! The main thing was that I was happy. My to-do list was getting longer and longer.

The priority now was to find a place to live. My own place! I liked the area that I was staying in and so wanted something within the vicinity.

I had to keep pinching myself to ensure that I wasn't dreaming. I exchanged numbers with Luca. He was going to schedule a meeting with his boss as soon as possible. I was glad that things were moving quickly; at least I would have some form of structure to my new life. Exciting times ahead for sure! Ethan was going to be busy with work for a few days which meant I would have to go flat hunting myself. This was a complete first for me as I was either living at home with family or living out of a suitcase. I had no idea of where to start looking so I asked Ethan who said the best and more reliable place to look for accommodation is in the local newspaper, 'Gulf News' which has a section for housing, jobs and everything you could possibly need. We parted about midnight. I was way too excited to sleep but I needed to be fresh for my challenge. However, there was something I needed to do when I got home. I rummaged through my hand luggage bag to find my paperwork. Flicking through and there it was staring right at me, my flight ticket to go home. I took it out of the pile and ripped it up into small pieces. I had to go the whole way, so goodbye to my ticket back to England. I threw the pieces in the air and danced around the room like I had won the lottery!

CHAPTER 5

Today seemed different but in a very positive way. I was full of beans which was just as well as I had a lot to do. Normally moving is a very stressful and tedious transaction but I was ready for this. First thing on the list was to buy the Gulf News. A full-on breakfast before doing anything was a must just in case I got too busy to eat later. I didn't want to stay in the hotel for another night if possible. I knew I was putting more pressure on myself but it was the only way to get things done.

So, after breakfast I took a quick trip to my usual coffee place and then to find a place to live. Yes, to live and not to stay for short term. The shock of everything moving so quickly was great energy fuel.

It was a beautiful sunny day as always so where better to flat search than sitting beside the fountain in Nasser square with my newspaper? It was fairly quiet, due to it being early as the day normally starts later here. I fast forwarded to the housing section and there was quite a selection of properties available for rent immediately. There was what looked like an amazing property on Sheikh Zayed Road which is the main highway running through Dubai. Ok, it was a bit out in the woods but from the photographs the place looked like a dream. A beautiful apartment on the tenth floor for a sky scraper building with magnificent views! What was unbelievable was the price of only £300 per month all in. That was a bargain. Maybe it was a spelling error. After exhausting all the possible reasons as to why it was too cheap I came to the conclusion that it must be the going rate for Dubai. After all it was written in black and white. I called the number and spoke with the flat owner. He was very enthusiastic over the phone and assured me that there was no error on the price. I made an appointment for a viewing which would be in couple of hours. Must be beginner's luck!

It was always good not to put all your eggs in one basket so I continued to look for other places. Another one that attracted my attention was a studio literally about five minute's walk from where I was sitting. It was more expensive at roughly £500 all in for the month. This didn't make sense to me as the cheaper accommodation was in an elite part of town. I called to book a viewing for this studio too.

The landlord was happy for me to come in the evening to view it, which meant I hadn't hit my target of moving out tonight. It was quite ambitious of me to think that I could do that in the first place. The main thing was to keep going.

As I continued to flick through my paper a man wearing the long robe decided to sit on the same bench as me. I didn't mind but all the other benches were vacant, so why was mine so special? I was sat on the right side of the bench and this person was sat at the end on the left side of the bench. I was reading the newspaper with quiet intensity and the guy kept fidgeting and seemed restless. We exchanged glances and trust me I didn't have my happy face on whereas he was all smiles. I carried on minding my own business until I heard a strange noise. I looked over and he was sat cross-legged facing me with his robe quite far up exposing himself. What made it more traumatic was that he was very excited down below and wearing only a smile by this time. I was flabbergasted. I didn't know where to look or what to do. My jaw had comfortably reached the floor. I clung on to my newspaper, got up and made a sharp exit. I could not have predicted that in a million years. What the hell was all that about? As I headed towards the taxi stand, the realisation of what just happened kicked in and I burst into fits of laughter like a child. I must have looked so ridiculous just laughing out loud to myself. Never a dull moment! To be fair I am a freak magnet, they find me no matter where I am, be it on the telephone or in the streets. Why was I so shocked? Lol!

My first flat viewing! What a feeling. It was very difficult to put in words. Truly a very surreal feeling! Luckily the traffic wasn't too stressful as had it been any later in the day, it would have taken me three times longer to get there.

The building was hugely impressive from the outside, no doubt. I called the landlord to say I was here. I got into the lift which was mirrored from top to bottom with such ornate designs on the rest of the tiles. It was luxurious. This really was me. I could imagine myself coming out of this building every day and saying to myself I live here. The lift was very high tech indeed as I was up on the tenth floor in no time. Door number ten was on the left as I exited the lift. There was a very smartly dressed man just outside the door. We made our introductions and went straight inside. The photographs did no justice to this apartment. It was magical, huge windows with a lot of natural light coming through. There even was a balcony with a cute little table and two chairs. I instantly pictured myself chilling out on the balcony watching the world go by.

It was spotless which seemed to be the known thing for Dubai.

They obviously took cleaning very seriously and to the ultimate level. The bathroom was a very reasonable size with a bath tub and shower. The living room was very spacious and minimal, just the way I like it.

Modern décor with a touch of Arabic essence! It was simply perfect. Now to the bedroom, again very spacious with ample wardrobes, a great big window and balcony too! This was the one for me for sure. There were two double beds in the room. One looked more used than the other. He asked me where I was from what I was doing here. The usual drill! He was a very pleasant guy. I asked him if he lived close by. He said 'very' with a smirk on his face. He said that he was going to be living in the flat with me. The bed near the window would be his and mine near the wardrobes. I was speechless. It wasn't sinking in so I asked him again. Basically, I would be room sharing. I think not. I had practically moved in there in my mind. How disappointing! Another sharp exit!

As I was waiting for the lift to come up, it all seemed to make sense. I mean why would anyone put up luxury apartment for rent for so little? It just was not meant to be. I felt disheartened for a short while but then managed to pull myself together. I had another viewing to go to. I had to keep positive.

It seemed like a perfect time to eat so as soon as I got out of the building I went in search for the dirtiest chicken and chips I could find. None in sight, just my luck! The next best thing was a Subway. It had to be a full foot sandwich dripping with every sauce they had and a large coke. Followed by a choc chip cookie!

I had to share my story with someone so called up Ethan who picked up the phone. He was crying with laughter at the other end. They say it happens in threes. What was next in line for me? A dreadful thought indeed. I kept the conversation short and headed back to the hotel. I thought it would be a good idea to pack my belongings as my days at the hotel were numbered.

There wasn't much to pack. I always liked to be organised and have everything in order to avoid cluttering the mind. It didn't take long at all. All nice and tidy! I needed some caffeine especially after the sort of day I was having. I got the coffee, knocked it back like a shot and headed to my second and last viewing of the day.

I wasn't too sure exactly where it was. I followed the instructions the landlord had sent me and surprisingly enough ended up at the right place.

He messaged me to say that he was going to be a bit late due to a hectic back log of work in his office. The location was worlds apart from the other property.

It was very much like being in the hub of wholesalers selling electrics, car parts and that kind of thing. A bit strange, but still, the buildings looked nice.

There he was, Faizel the landlord. He walked briskly in my direction and took me towards the stairs of the building where the studio was situated. Only two floors up and we were there. The hallway was bit a dark and grim covered in dark grey tiles. Not to my taste at all. It looked like a really old un-used hotel lobby. Left from the lift a few doors down, there was number nine. He tried to find the keys out of a bunch of what looked like hundreds. I was waiting anxiously. At last he found the right one and opened the door. As you walked in there was a kitchenette on your left. A bit further down, the bathroom was a reasonable size with a power shower, and then there was the main living space which was a good size and included a wardrobe, big mirror, television near a massive window and then a double sized bed. I don't know why but I got an instant good feeling about the place and shook on the deal with Faizel. I had done it. I found a home in a short space of time. I was totally ecstatic! It just had that homely feel and I know I would make it my own with bits and pieces. There even was cutlery, pots and pans in the cupboard so I was all set to go. It was decided that I would move in two days as it needed a lick of paint and a good clean. I was a very happy man.

As soon as I left the building I messaged both Ethan and Luca who could not believe the speed I was working at. I am a firm believer that if anything needs to be done do it today because tomorrow never comes. Luca still hadn't mentioned anything about having words with his bosses about me. I really needed the work now especially that I had committed myself to living here, but maybe it was best to wait a little bit longer. I decided I would remind him once I was all settled in my new home.

It was impossible to try and sleep now. The excitement was too overwhelming. I was quite proud of myself, I must admit. I must have fallen asleep very late as I was shattered in the morning. I was so reluctant to get up. There was no rush for anything today. It was tomorrow that would be a crazy day as that was when the big move was happening. It would be nice to go shopping for a few homely things. Amidst all this I had forgotten one very important thing and that was to tell my family that I was not coming back. I decided it was best to wait till I had secured some work as I wanted to show them I had a foundation here and that I meant business.

The day of the move finally arrived. It was very straight forward. Just a suitcase, hand bag and a couple of carrier bags! Faizel was already waiting for me at the apartment bright and early. He went through some of the formalities at a good pace then handed me the keys. He showed himself out. Another chapter in my life was beginning. The plan for today was to settle into my new home and relax. I had bought a metal key ring of the UAE flag from the gift shop just a few meters away. My house keys were about to be christened. I also noticed on my way in there was a large supermarket just a few yards away. Very handy!

Before unpacking I thought it wise to have a full on cleaning session everywhere even though the landlord had a cleaner in. I grabbed my wallet and keys and headed to the supermarket. I needed some marigolds and every type of spray. It's always good to be organised. It literally took me two minutes to get to the supermarket. I filled my basket up mainly with cleaning products, some milk, tea bags and other essentials. Every so often I would get this reminder that I was living in Dubai now and it automatically put a big smile on my face. I put on my pyjama suit with my sexy gloves and was ready to get on all fours to scrub the day away. In all fairness, it didn't take too long as it wasn't the biggest studio. It was hugely satisfying to know that it had been cleaned to my standards.

Cleaning done, now time to unpack! The clothes fitted in perfectly in the wardrobe as it was so tall and spacious. It was big enough for me to fit in so I tested it. I fitted in perfectly. It was really looking cosy and homely now. Everything was in its place. My model portfolios would be resting on the sideboard.

I must admit I was really tired. The amazing thing about living in Dubai was not just the heat and how exotic it was but the fact I could order my groceries with just a phone call and they would deliver to my doorstep for free of charge. That would be unheard of in the UK. Not only groceries but the same rules applied to fast food places and restaurants too. There was no way I was going to cook today so I decided to order in a spicy chicken wrap meal. They said it would take fifteen minutes and I got it in ten.

I had a reasonably early night. As I lay down in my head I felt an itch. I was too tired and ignored it. This itching however continued for a few days and there was proof in the lumpy spots all over my body that something was not quite right. I freaked out! I needed to take a trip to the pharmacy ASAP. Then one night I got up to go to the toilet and on my way, I saw two beastly looking cockroaches.

They were abnormally big and so vicious looking. It's almost like they had a face of victory after having bitten me several times.

I had to report this to the landlord. As soon as morning arrived I was on the telephone. I was lucky that he understood my situation as he reassured me that it would be taken care of that very day. The only thing was that I would have to make myself scarce for the day as the apartment would be fumigated. What a pain. It was for my own good. At least I could go to the pharmacy, pick up my trousers from the tailors without rushing. I was hoping this was the third and final thing to go wrong!

The day was moving quite swiftly. I ended up having a large lunch at the Indian quarters of Dubai, Meena Bazaar. It was definitely a day for something very meaty and spicy. I found a tiny little random restaurant hidden away. It was quiet and clean, just what I needed. The menu was extensive and so cheap. I ordered my chicken curry and naan bread. The presentation was not all that great but the flavours were divine. Succulent chicken fell off the bone in a thick spicy sauce swept up with the best fresh bread ever. The style was very much on home cooking. I then collected my trousers from the tailors. They were such a great fit. I like quirky things and I had every confidence that the tailors would be able to create all my unusual clothing collections. I got home and as I entered I was hit with the residue of the smoke even though the windows were fully open. It would just take some time to settle.

It was coming towards the end of my third week in Dubai, can't believe that time was going too quickly. My family didn't contact me to ask why I was there longer than two weeks which was the original plan. They would have known I was having too much of a good time. They were great like that, just leaving me to my own devices.

The thing is that my visa was only valid for thirty days. I had no idea how I could renew it. I called Luca as he had been in Dubai for a very long time and seemed very clued up on these things. He seemed very apologetic when I spoke to him as he still hadn't been able to speak to anyone about me as his boss had some family emergency. I asked him what I needed to do as my visa was running out. He said it was quite simple, all I needed to do was to fly out to the nearest country which was Oman, get my passport stamped and come back. That was the only way at that time. It wasn't as simple as walking into an office and getting a stamp. That would give me another thirty days to play with. Hopefully by that time I would have a great job and my employers would be the ones that would have to deal with the headache of sorting my visa as per the rule. I was quickly learning all the ins and outs of living in the UAE.

My next project was to book a flight to Oman, Muscat. It's only forty-five minutes away so not too bad. A few days later I went to the travel agent which was situated near the fish roundabout on Al Makhtoum Road, again just a nice short stroll away. The reason why it's called the fish roundabout is quite obvious as there are a couple of giant fish sculptures in the middle of the roundabout with water dribbling over them. It was a great landmark. Thankfully the travel agent was very quiet and I was attended to straight away. It was costing me the equivalent to £50 for a return ticket to Oman so not bad at all. My flight was booked for three days later.

It was a great feeling that I had settled in so quickly and was so familiar with my routes. I knew my area really well and had acknowledged all the amenities around me. Still not having cooked a single thing at home, I decided to carry on this trend for as long as possible even though I love cooking. I discovered another hidden gem. It was the smallest Chinese restaurant I have ever seen. I ordered a chilly chicken peanut curry and rice. The waiter gave me some chopsticks and there was not a fork in sight. That was all fine however I had never eaten with chopsticks before. I really didn't know what to do with them. There was always a first time. I must have managed a grain at a time. The food was so scrumptious. As if by magic I was beginning to get a good grip of the chopsticks. Still not perfect but getting there slowly. It was a good excuse to keep coming to that restaurant. A nice little challenge to get stuck in to!

I was excited by the journey ahead of me today. It was just a shame that I wouldn't be able to venture out into Oman. I got to the airport in good time. It wasn't much of a trek. There didn't seem that many people boarding on my flight. Time to board and as I approached the aeroplane I could not believe how small it was. The capacity was only two people on either side. It was a very intimate flight. By the time we were in the air it was time to descend. It was just a case of when the aeroplane would land, I would need to literally go through the airport get my stamp and sit back on the same plane again to go back to Dubai. I learnt that all the passengers that day were doing the same as me, renewing their visas. Quite a cool way to do it, better than having to wait in an office for hours on end! Thankfully that wasn't an option!

It was time to put on my serious hat. I was spending a lot of money but not earning anything. The money I had was not going to last forever so I came up with a great idea. There was no reason why I couldn't start modelling here.

I know every country has their own take on the industry but I didn't have anything to lose. I am a very experienced professional with several skills.

Now was the time to utilise them to the full. There was a great job section in the Gulf News. All the adverts, whether for jobs, accommodation, selling or buying things were 100% genuine. The laws were very strict and you would not be able to put any bogus advertisements up and get away with it, which was reassuring. The price to pay would be too phenomenal.

I was feeling confident that it wouldn't be long before I would be working as I had a very strong portfolio and drive to succeed. Nothing was going to stop me.

I picked up a copy of the Gulf News and that evening went through all the adverts. There was a lot on interesting work available. All paid work too. Smart phones had not been invented yet so it would be a case of taking a trip to the internet café and sending emails to potential employers. The modelling industry seemed to be picking up pace here and I managed to find a lot of agencies online. I sent my CV, photographs and my vital statistics to several model agencies and companies recruiting models and creative people. Surely something positive would come out of this, after all I was putting in the time. Whilst searching on the net, I came across a great editorial Arabic magazine called 'Arabian Man'. I loved the style of photography and decided to take a speculative approach and contact them directly to see if we could work together. I was beginning to understand that if I marketed myself in the correct manner, I seriously could do quite well for myself. Dubai was very fast developing in all industries and seemed to be at the centre of the world. Today was a very long but productive day. A strong cup of tea was well over due from the café around the corner from the flat. Why make tea yourself when you can get it made to perfection by someone else?

It was time to make my mark in the Arab world.

CHAPTER 6

It seemed like I was spending more and more time in the internet café than anywhere else. I am surprised they didn't start charging me rent. It was all for a good cause though. The rewards were starting to show. I got a reply from Arabian Man magazine. They were interested in meeting me. Being a real eager beaver I asked if it was possible to go in a bit later the same day. They said it was fine to come in around 4.30pm with my portfolio.

I had plenty of time and so wanted to take a little boat ride across to Bur Dubai again. It really was a very pleasant trip. I wanted to venture out into mini Mumbai (Meena Bazaar) so headed out. It seemed hotter than normal. I considered this as a daily blessing. As soon as I stepped off the boat I was offered perfumes, watches, designer bags, clothes all original fakes of course. If the sellers were to get caught the punishment would be extremely severe. They were quite happy taking risks besides they had a talent for spotting foreigners who were their prime target market. You could dress like a local, talk like a local but they would suss you out in no time. Besides locals would never ever be seen wearing anything fake. That would be blasphemous! I managed to neatly manoeuvre around the traders and ended up in a traditional Indian clothing shop. I was talked into looking at some funky menswear outfits normally worn at weddings. I certainly didn't have a wedding to go to, not in the near future. He was a great salesman and talked me into trying an outfit that I showed a keen interest in. It was a three-piece black suit comprising a long black jacket with silver hand embroidered detail around the neck, the waistcoat had some beautiful embroidery down the front of it and trousers which were normal straight cut and pleated at the waist. It was a perfect fit, as if it had been made for me but I didn't dare ask the price. It was without doubt a designer piece. So, I took the plunge and asked him the price. He came up with the equivalent of £375. There was no way I was paying that much. To be honest I didn't even want the outfit. So, I said 'no' point blank and then he asked how much I would be willing to pay. Being the king of bartering, it was my time to shine and use my skills. I said to him I was only willing to pay £75. I stuck by that. I told him I was a model and that I would tell everyone where I got the outfit from. I had to try. I think he knew he was fighting a losing battle and so agreed. It was my bargain of the day. He packed my outfit and he said that I should work in sales. I said thanks but no thanks and headed out.

There was a bit of a wait for the boat to leave, so the queues to get on it were building up fast. I sat right at the front so the sun would shine directly in my face. We headed out and as we got about half way I noticed a man looking at me and laughing. Then a group of them that were initially talking to each other turned their faces towards me. They broke into fits of laughter. It was like the domino effect. Eventually the whole boat was looking at me and laughing their heads off. It wasn't making any sense. Naturally I became very paranoid and disembarked as soon as it stopped. I had a good fifteen minute-walk to get home, through the main square and past all the shops. Eventually I reached home. I threw my bags on the bed and just happened to catch a glimpse of myself in the mirror. I wished that the ground could have swallowed me up. It all made sense now. So, this was why the strangers on the boat were so amused. My whole face was covered in soot from the engine revving. It was as if I were wearing a black mask. The only white bits were my teeth and the white in my eyes. I looked like a freak.

Recovering from my ordeal, it was time to get all dressed up to go for my casting which was on Sheikh Zayed Road. I looked good and felt confident and was totally ready to rock. I had two model portfolios, one for commercial modelling, and the other for high fashion editorial. I noticed I had about three missed calls from Luca. I didn't have time to chat now. It would be best to speak to him once I had the casting out of the way.

In the taxi, I got my books ready. This could really do wonders for my career. It would give me the exposure I needed, being a newbie on the block. I entered the office. It was quite dull in the way it was decorated. Not very inspiring to be honest! The receptionist called one of the editors to let them know of my arrival. A tall very unfashionable man walked through the door into the main reception area and very coldly shook my hand. Being the professional that I am, I introduced myself and then handed him my portfolios. He said he wanted to show his colleagues. I felt a very negative vibe flawing through the air. I could hear him talk about me and he wasn't saying nice things. He was speaking in Hindi which I understand fully.

He said that I should do make up shoots only and nothing else and that I don't even look like a man in the photographs. He said I would not make it as a model in Dubai and that I should stop wasting people's time. Then he started laughing like someone had told him the funniest joke. It became more of a personal thing than constructive criticism.

As a model, you became very thick skinned as people are very critical. You cannot take things to heart. I am a professional and have worked in the industry for many years and am completely aware of my strengths and weaknesses. The tone of voice this man spoke in was of very malicious. I have a very versatile look and am quite happy testing out different looks. As models, that is our job. We are a blank canvas that can be moulded into anything. In my book, the photographs that the editor was referring to were from a shoot I did with a very prestigious fashion photographer which were used for various things. These photographs had got me a lot of work. How dare he speak to me like that? He was far from professional. Let's be honest, he would never get work anywhere else in the world with that kind of stinking attitude. He obviously had no idea how the industry worked in the mainstream. I firmly requested to have my books back and left the building. I was still in shock. It was fine if I was not suitable for the magazine but there were politer ways of saying 'no!' It really was not a good start to things. I had to keep my chin up and keep going. I had made the sacrifice of choosing this new life so I had to see it through. It was proving much tougher than I had imagined.

On the way back, I called Luca. I had to moan to him about my horrific experience. He told me there were many more opportunities out there and that I was worth so much more. He also said he wanted to meet up a bit later in the evening as he had some interesting news for me. He assured me it was all positive. That's all I needed to hear after that experience. Luca was presenting some show about the Shopping Festival, which takes place twice a year, in winter for a couple of months and in summer too. This is basically the equivalent to the sales that we have in the UK. Everything in the shops is reduced to a ridiculous amount. This festival is taken quite seriously as on the television they run the most amazing competitions where you can win cars, villas, more cars and a substantial amount of money. It really is worth participating as the stakes are high. It would be nice to experience this and enjoy the atmosphere. I was looking forward to meeting up with Luca. I hope he has managed to get me a good work contract. I really need to be buckling down and working as my money was going so quickly.

I went home to get some rest. It was truly needed. I think I was adjusting well and at a good pace. I must have nodded off for about two hours. I quickly got dressed and headed out to a coffee shop in Al Rigga which was not too far from Beirut restaurant. It was nice to see a familiar face. After another summarised moaning session, it was time to talk business.

Luca said that he had put in a good word for me at the office saying that I am very professional and very experienced and that I would be great in working on some of the English lifestyle programmes. His boss was convinced I would be a great candidate for the job. I would be presenting, researching and producing programmes.

This was exactly what I needed to hear! I could have screamed the place down in excitement, I was so happy. I was so grateful to Luca and kept thanking him for his kindness in putting me forward for this position. Apparently, it's a known thing in Dubai, that the best way to get a job is on recommendation. I would have to go to the office the following day to fill out all the necessary forms and get the formalities out of the way so that they could work on getting my visa sorted. This was really exciting. Today was a day for celebrations. Dinner was on me, no arguments. Luca reluctantly agreed.

We decided to order food from the coffee shop as we had both got too comfortable in our seats. It was noisy, even though it was quite late at night. The conversations were nice and chilled out and then I asked him about his situation here. He seemed very settled in every way in Dubai but I was most intrigued by his background as he was Lebanese. Lebanon is known as the Milan of the Middle East as people are very liberal, cultured and fashionable. It's a place I have always wanted to visit so I wondered why he chose to settle in Dubai. He said he needed a change and that he was getting a much better deals financially in Dubai. It was an offer he couldn't refuse. I didn't even know where he was living so I asked him.

He said he was based in Sharjah which on a good day can be a half an hour drive. On a bad day, it could easily take triple the amount of time. He liked the quietness and the less hectic lifestyle.

Unfortunately, he would have to leave his swanky flat as the owner didn't want tenants anymore. He looked quite stressed as we talked about his housing situation. He didn't have anywhere lined up due to lack of time. I felt really bad for him, so me being me offered to let him stay with me until he got himself sorted. I felt so appreciative that he was helping me with my work situation. It was the least I could do. He kept saying that he didn't want to put me out, but I insisted. He finally agreed, but only if he could contribute towards the rent. He was insistent, so we agreed on him contributing towards the rent. He still had a few days on his tenancy in which to sort himself out and pack his belongings which was good because I needed to get organised too.

It had been another constructive evening. Tonight was the night. I had to do the deed and tell my family of my master plan. I had put it off enough times and now that I had a job in place I had no reason to delay it further.

I got home roughly about midnight and as soon as I got in I called my mum. Everyone was at my grandmother's house, perfect timing! I could do it all in one go. I managed to speak to everyone which was nice as it made me realise that I did miss my family even though I had been caught up with my new life. Naturally they were wondering why I hadn't come back yet so this was a good point to go into the details. I broke the news to my grandmother first and said that a great work opportunity has come up and I was going to stay until the contract came to an end. I could really sense the sadness in her voice which naturally was upsetting to me. I reassured her that I was well and very happy with my decision. I know she was equally happy for me. She put my mum on the phone and then my sister. I knew it was going to be a difficult but it had to be done.

Still feeling upset at the thought of not seeing my family for a while I diverted my attention to the following day. Since it was contract signing day it was going to be very special. On that happy note, I nodded off all cosy and comfortable in my bed.

Morning came around quickly. The excitement was mounting up, thick and fast. It was a big day. I had waited a long time for this. Finally, it was unfolding into reality. As normal, I bathed myself with my favourite scents. The smell of success! My appointment at the office was 2pm. It was a bit of a trek as it was at the Media city in Jebel Ali which was still along the main highway but much further down; a good forty-minute drive. In the short time I had been in Dubai, I don't think I had ever sat in so many taxis. It was nice to be driven. At least I could get myself together and focus on the meeting.

In true Nadeem style, I turned up 1:30pm. I am always early wherever I go. I hate being late; it's almost like having a phobia. The reception area was quite small. No one was around. It felt very empty and a bit lifeless. Luca called me to his office. He requested to see my passport and took a photocopy of it. He then pulled out a long form what I assumed was an application form. The thing was it was all in Arabic. I couldn't make heads or tail of it so I asked him if I could have an English version. He said no and not to worry and that he would fill most of it in, all I had to do was sign in the appropriate places. Normally I would be more inquisitive and ask more questions but I trusted him and signed it without hesitation. Once it was all signed and sealed he said that I needed to pay the equivalent of £500 cash as this will be for all the admin work and for the visa itself. That's a lot of money to put up front. Was it going to be presented in a gold frame or something? I wasn't too impressed. I thought it was the responsibility of the employer to sort it.

He assured me that initially I would have to bear the costs but when the renewal would come up the employer would take care of it. So, without a further thought I paid the £500. I asked him when I would get it and he replied saying that it can take a good two weeks. The turnover was much slower there. I had waited all this time for an opportunity like this so what was another two weeks? I didn't get a copy of any of the paperwork but I didn't think much of it. I left the office much poorer than I started off. I kept telling myself it was an investment towards my career, and that's priceless. Just as I was about to call the lift, Luca came running out. He said he would be moving in the following day. That was both good and bad. On one hand, he would be contributing towards the rent which would be help me. However, I hoped he wasn't going to be staying too long as I like my own space.

My life was supposed to get *more* exciting by the day, not the opposite. For now, it was time to wear the rubber gloves and get scrubbing yet again. I cleaned everything inside out and was happy with the outcome so decided to treat myself to a full on Chinese meal at my usual place. It was really busy. I asked for my normal meal which was the spicy chicken peanut curry. I also asked them for chopsticks. I wanted to perfect the art of using them. I opted for a takeaway as I fancied a TV dinner. Even though I couldn't understand or speak much Arabic I was getting engrossed in a Syrian soap that was on every day. It was the Arabic equivalent of Eastenders. I really loved the music channel too and became addicted to the sounds. Such provocative dance beats and catchy tunes. Even the videos were really enticing! I was certainly becoming more cultured.

I hadn't checked my emails in a few days and so wondered off to the net café after polishing off my dinner and becoming more fluent in using chopsticks. To my delight I had received a lot of replies from agencies. Five out of seven wanted to sign me up. I was so happy. It felt like light at the end of the tunnel. In fact, one of the agencies was already asking my availability for a job. It was for Mac Makeup. The job was to model different looks on the catwalk. It's quite ironic that I should get this job after my experience with the magazine people. It was paying quite well too, in the region of about £500 for the day. I couldn't believe my luck. The location was a real selling point. It was going to be held in the middle of the desert. Double wow! I needed to call the agent in the morning as she stated that I needed to go into the office.

Even though I was booked, they needed to make sure that I looked more-or-less the same as my pictures as I had been booked on those grounds.

I took my portfolios to the agency which was situated in a very unusual shaped building. It looked like a pyramid. It was so sleek and unique. The agent was more than happy with my look and we were good to go. The event was to take place on the Thursday, only two days away. Thursday is the beginning of the weekend in the Middle East. This was a sure way to start the weekend on a real high for me. We would get picked up at a meeting point and be driven down and dropped back at the same point. They assured me we would be fed and very well looked after. That was always good to hear. It also confirmed the professionalism of the agency. However, I was still not 100% sure what I'd be doing. To be honest I was counting my blessings so was not too concerned. The risk of being asked to run naked through the desert was pretty low. It was beginning to happen all at once. I was on a real high.

Luca moved in on the Tuesday evening. To my surprise he came with very minimal belongings. He said it was ok to store his things in the garage of the other place until he was ready to collect them. I was so used to having the space to myself that it felt weird having to share it. I was feeling in the mood for a bit of cooking and so placed my order for the groceries over the phone. Shortly afterwards, there was a knock at the door and my groceries arrived. It was sheer laziness on my part, but if you can then why not? The menu was much improvised. I had some onion, garlic, green peppers, chilli powder, Frankfurt chicken sausages and some freshly baked Lebanese bread. All I did was chop everything up into tiny pieces, added chilli, salt and fresh lemon juice. I then heated some oil in the wok and added all the ingredients in and cooked it till it was lightly brown. It tasted amazing with the bread. Very random indeed!

I had heard about the Global Village and really wanted to go. It was an area where they have exhibitions of food, trinkets and clothes from around the globe; all very authentic. There were lots of stands housed under one roof and apparently you literally got a taste from different countries. Luckily Luca was off work which meant I had some company.

Having used taxis for the majority of the time, I wanted to experience getting around in a bus, and why not? Not only are they efficient and air conditioned but very cheap too. It's always good to try different things. That's always been my motto. It was quite a smooth and comfortable ride. However they were no signs of any queuing systems.

A good push and tug was the only chance you had if you wanted to get on as the buses are over-crowded. It felt quite uncivilised which was a bit shocking to the system. If you can't beat them, join them!

We managed to get on and off in one piece. As we headed into the thick of the action I completely understood what all the fuss was about. It was so vibrant, like a kaleidoscope. All the countries were under one roof. It was like being on a set of a film. I felt transported into another world. All the exhibitors were offering food samples. I did not refuse any. They were such warm and polite people. I felt I was being highly educated in so many different cultures. We walked around the stands and came to the Lebanese stand. Luca seemed very familiar with the guy there. He said they both were neighbours in Lebanon and have known each other for many years. He was a very happy chappy kind of guy. His name was Maher. He spoke amazing English so conversing was easy. The only thing I found odd was that they kept on talking in Arabic which I considered to be highly rude. If he was able to speak in English then what was the problem? We must have been with Maher for a good thirty minutes. I wanted to cover most of the exhibitions so we continued to plough through. It was a very enjoyable experience.

My phone was buzzing and messages were coming in from Ethan who seemed to have gone quiet for some time. He said that he had been really busy with work and said that he wanted to stay over on Friday night. I would have appreciated it if he would have asked me first rather than enforcing his decision. It was just bad manners. I was in no mood to push it. He said we could celebrate me moving to Dubai and having my own place. All I wanted was a quiet life. That wasn't happening for sure.

I didn't want to have much of a late night as it was my first day at work the following day. I wanted to look fresh and kick ass! With every job I do, I wanted to give it my all and make a good impression as this could lead into all sorts of fascinating directions.

CHAPTER 7

It was the first day at work after what felt like forever. I enjoyed working and liked to be consistent with it. Thank God it wasn't an early start. Me and my fellow colleagues who I hadn't even seen yet or knew of were told to meet on Sheikh Zayed Road outside TGI Fridays at 2pm. It was so exciting and slightly nerve wracking at the same time. My first job in Dubai! Different countries have different ways of working but as long as these guys were professional and treated us well as they said they would, then it was all good.

I had a good wholesome breakfast to kick start the day as I knew it was going to be a very lengthy one. All charged up with my caffeine I was ready to hit the road. It was always a very pleasant journey in the taxis as I would always befriend the driver for a short while. For once I was not the only one there early. A very stunning tall Arabic female model had beaten me. She was from Lebanon and had come to Dubai to pursue her modelling career dream. She was doing extremely well from what I learnt. Affra was her name. Then one by one they all piled in. All very different and each model as strong as the other! It almost felt like being a contestant for a beauty pageant being surrounded by all these beautiful people. Eventually the agent strolled in with her hands full of bags struggling with the weight of them. She introduced herself and then was prepping herself for the briefing session.

We were to be given harem pants which are baggy trousers cuffed at the ankle with a transparent tunic for the boys and short cropped tops for the girls. We would all have to have our makeup done by one of the many makeup artists, then move onto the hair stylist. Then came the best bit, our job was to walk down with very strong faces up and down, go backstage wash our faces and get them painted again and that was it! What an easy job. She also said that once the show was done we could enjoy the rest of the evening. In a nutshell, it was all about strutting and chilling. I could live with that. I loved doing catwalk shows. I was good at keeping a very serious face and walking in a much stylised fashion, so I was totally in my element.

We all got onto a very luxury coach which was to take us to the desert, a journey which would take around forty minutes. By this time everyone was getting to know one another and we all seemed very comfortable with each other which is always a great thing. There is nothing worse than working with a stuck-up model who thinks they are more superior to others!

As we approached closer to our destination it was time to switch vehicles and get into a 4x4. They were several vehicles waiting for us as not only were we driven to the location but the guests coming to the event would be chauffeur driven too. This is the kind of hospitality that Dubai offers. Finally, everyone was in their allocated vehicle. The driver had just let the air out of the tyres which is what they apparently do when entering the desert. All set, here we go. Luckily, I sat in the front seat. I had never done a desert safari before and this ride would be a great taster of what it's about. I was like a child laughing away as we skidded in the sand then climbing the sand dunes at high speed. What a fantastic experience. I was so amazed at how the driver knew exactly where to go as I couldn't see any markings or anything that would indicate what direction we needed to head in. We were getting closer to the patch where we were going to be stationed. I could see the stage designers at work; it was going to be quite a spectacular event.

They were building a Bedouin camp with real flame torches with all the trimmings including the Arabic lanterns, the drapes and a walk way for us to strutt our stuff. Not to forget a changing area for us all. I was so overwhelmed with the manpower for this event. They were building at the speed of light and there it was a beautiful authentic Bedouin camp. To keep the flow of the authenticity it was all floor seating. I was looking forward to the food as a full barbeque was on the menu.

I put my belongings in the changing area and stepped out to feel the warm breeze and the coolness of the sand on my feet. I breathed in the fresh air. It was so liberating and therapeutic. All the stresses of life simply melted away. It was a beautiful feeling of ecstasy, so soothing and healing as I felt the cool warm air hit my face. This truly was a very special moment in my life. I had to come back down to earth as we were being allocated our outfits and the makeup artist was eagerly waiting to work her magic on my face. The outfit was quite cool and went with the theme of the evening. It's not that I had a choice anyway. The makeup was however very full on. To the point where I was sure that the male models had more makeup on than the girls. The look was very traditional Arabic with strong black eyes and flawless skin. A great look for the stage and the stage only! The evening was racing ahead. We all stood in line to do our walk. I was the first model. My facial expression changed from being all happy and cheery to a serious model look with a killer pout. There I went rocking the catwalk. The interaction from the crowds was fantastic. One more walk and then I could enjoy stuffing my face and start networking.

Back in my normal clothes, feeling human again as the makeup artist washed away all her hard work from my face. The music was getting louder and more club like. The podium dancers came on and did their thing. I was cheering at the top of my lungs to show my support. I could smell the food making its way in my direction. Thank goodness it was self-service as I piled up my plate with succulent kebabs, hummus and fresh salad. It tasted incredible. Even though I was full to the core there was most certainly room for desert which was Om Ali the Arabic equivalent to rice pudding. It was hot, creamy and full of nuts. A perfect finish to any meal! I chatted with as many people as possible. There were some very interesting people that had attended including local film makers, model agencies, fashion designers and so on. I really didn't feel like I had worked at all on this day. The fact I was paid for it made it feel that much more surreal.

The ride home in the desert was equally exhilarating. I must have got home just before midnight only to find Ethan there making himself very much at home. I wasn't expecting him there till the following day so why was he there? He said he managed to leave work early and so decided that he would surprise me with his presence. It was more of a shock as I had a long day and wanted to relax. As I had already eaten which they didn't know about, they were hungry. Luca hadn't even bothered to sort dinner which was highly annoying as I was always very thoughtful and made sure there was food in the fridge. A thought pondered in my mind and that was when he was going to leave. My space wasn't mine anymore and it was beginning to feel a bit crowded even though it had not been that long since Luca had moved in. I kept that thought to myself. I ordered some food for them from chicken cottage. I paid as no one else bothered to even offer.

Ethan said that we should have a party the following day with just the three of us. He said he would get some drinks in if I would provide some snacks. I wondered what he meant by drinks. I assumed there would be soft drinks, but no he mentioned alcohol too. I had never drunk any alcohol in my life even though I had always wondered what it tasted like and what all the fuss was about. Bearing that in mind I wasn't going to start drinking it any time now. The night rounded up quite quickly as I insisted on an early night because of my long day.

I had the best sleep that I can remember. I felt so much better for it. The others were up and making toast. I requested Luca to get some coffee from the café. It was a great way to start the day.

We were having general chit chat conversations and then it turned specifically to me, Luca mentioned that I needed to get my university certificates and any other educational certificates authenticated by getting them stamped at the UAE consulate in London. I was living in Dubai now. How would that be possible? I had brought my birth certificate, university certificate and proof of other courses I had completed in the UK with me. Why wasn't that enough? He said eventually I would need them to confirm my credentials. This was so annoying as nothing of this nature had been mentioned to me earlier.

This lead me onto the progression of my visa which had crossed my mind on several occasions but I had been side tracked with other things. Luca said that it was in process of being sorted and he wasn't sure how much longer it would take and that there was nothing to worry about. My job was safe! He suggested that maybe I should go back to the UK to sort my certificates as in the long run it would be worth my while. In a way, the idea was appealing if only so I could see my family and say good bye to all my friends and bring back more of my belongings. The frustrating thing was that I would also have to travel to London in order to get everything stamped. I guessed that was life.

It was the weekend and I had no intention of thinking of work or anything else that would worry my mind. We decided that after watching a bit of television we could start preparing for the so-called party later. The music channel was on and my favourite Arabic song was blasting out with the stunning Nancy Ajram with her track 'Ah We Noss'. Such a great catchy tune with a traditional funky vibe! The video is so memorable too! It shows her washing clothes looking like a typical Egyptian girl with hens running around and then she spots this guy checking her out, she checks him out and then he ends up following her and so on. Another one of my favourite tracks is 'Ad El Hob' by Katia Arb. More mellow but still addictive to listen to. Also, the next episode of my favourite Syrian soap was going to be on. I promised that we would make a move after that.

I was lucky that there were so many shops and amenities on my door step which meant very minimal travelling. I forced myself off the sofa and we all headed out. My eyes caught a pair of pointed beige shoes that were screaming my name. I went inside the shop and tried them on. They fitted so well so I treated myself to them. They weren't even expensive. Ethan got the exact same ones. It was nice walking around with no agenda. I spotted a man selling coconut water and ran in that direction as I love anything coconutty. It was so energising and tasted heavenly. I could have easily had about four more.

We headed towards the supermarket and I bought some chicken nuggets, falafels, koftas, fresh Lebanese bread and some ready-made salad. Finger food is quick and easy and I could not be bothered to make a full gourmet meal. I paid for my shopping then both Luca and Ethan said that I should head back home and that they would bring the drinks. I merrily strolled home. I was excited about having my flat to myself even though it would be for a short while. Anything was better than nothing.

I quickly put all the shopping away and threw myself on the bed. All that rushing around was seriously catching up. I fell into a deep sleep and sadly was woken up by a loud knock on the door. I had slept for about three hours and the boys had just come back now. I freshened up and started with the cooking, not that there was much to cook. It was a case of deep fat frying so not the healthiest of choices but a bit of unhealthy cannot do much harm.

By the time all the frying was done all the smell of the oil had happily seeped into my hair and clothes which meant I had to shower again. I told Luca to set the table with the food and have everything ready before I come out.

As I stepped out I saw the table was well spread with all the bits of food and plenty of cartons of orange juice, lemonade and the biggest bottle of Jack Daniels. We all sat around the table chilling out and enjoying the moment. Ethan finally did the honours and started pouring out the drinks. I insisted that I was only going to have a soft drink. I had previously made it clear that I don't drink. Ethan had bought three pint-size glasses and made a drink for himself and Luca. Quite a healthy portion of Jack Daniels to orange juice! The smell of it was disgusting. He asked if he should make me a drink and I blatantly said no. He insisted and I persisted that I didn't want to try any alcohol. He then said well how will you know what it's like if you have never tasted it. To be fair I had always wondered what the effects of alcohol was and what it tasted like. I was away from home and always very curious so why shouldn't I give it a try? That way I would be out of my misery once and for all. So hesitantly I said yes.

He then poured me a very generous amount. I didn't need to drink all of it anyway. We said a big 'cheers' and I took my first ever sip. It tasted vile so I got Ethan to add more orange juice. It was still disgusting in taste but a bit more bearable. I was fine and couldn't feel any effects yet. I felt absolutely normal. Then that was it. I don't recall much else of that evening apart from a few unpleasant snippets like being pushed into the shower with my clothes on by Ethan.

The water gushing down my face whilst I was crying like a baby! I also remember the louder I cried the harder he slapped me on my face. He then left me alone whilst I continued to cry. The next horrific moment is that I reached into the cupboard and smashed the plates onto the floor. It was like production line, one plate smashed and the other plate was ready and waiting to be smashed in my other hand. Again, Ethan came and slapped me so hard that I fell on the floor. The rest is a complete blur.

I woke up in the morning feeling so unwell. My head was pounding. I found myself on the floor. I very slowly lifted myself up. My clothes still feeling very damp. As my eyes opened wider I had the biggest shock of my life. The floor was covered in pieces of smashed plates and food. There wasn't a clean spot in sight. I managed to walk over to the sofa and tried to get comfortable but my head would not let me. My whimpering got louder which finally woke up Luca and Ethan. I needed an explanation of what happened. Ethan said I got completely drunk and was not in my senses at all. He tried to calm me down but I was uncontrollable and that why he slapped me several times. It was the first time my body had consumed any alcohol. Naturally I was going to have some kind of reaction. I tried to fight my case but was feeling too unwell. I learnt that I officially had my first hangover. I felt hugely ashamed and disgusted with myself. How could I have dropped to this level? It made me realise that alcohol was definitely not for me. That would be the first and last time. The effects of the aftermath were enough to put me off for life.

That day all I did was sleep hoping that I would feel normal again. I was told as I had made the mess it was up to me to clear it up which I was happy to do because I was still feeling horrified by what I had done. The embarrassment didn't end there as I had severely vomited in the bathroom sink and blocked it. I had to call for the care taker of the building to come and see to the sink. He came in very eager to sort the problem. I admitted it was me who had caused the damage and I could not apologise enough for my stupidity. He was so nice bless him, without thinking twice stuck his bare hands in my vomit to clear it up and started rummaging through. This just made me feel sick even more. He eventually unblocked it. I thanked him continuously as he made his way out. I was left to clear up the mess by myself, but before anything else it was time for another nap living in hope that I would feel normal again soon!

CHAPTER 8

A few days on and I was still in recovery from my horrific drinking ordeal. I was feeling more normal each day thankfully. The really odd thing was that Ethan ended up staying on much longer than expected; a whole three days extra. I found this really disrupting as I couldn't concentrate on what I needed to do. The list was getting longer and I was getting more forgetful. I was planning my trip back to Accrington. The more I thought about it the more excited I grew. Naturally I was missing my family but not to the extent where I would move back to the UK. I hadn't come with the intention of staying more permanently so I hadn't been able to say goodbye to my friends or my family properly. I also needed more clothing and other bits too.

I went to the travel agents later that day in Bur Dubai to book my ticket back to the UK. I managed to get a direct flight for a reasonable price. I would only be away for seven nights. My money was surely running low now. I still didn't get any financial help from Luca. I wasn't sure how to tackle this situation and decided that I needed to confront him about this. He had not contributed to a single thing. I could never do that to anyone, especially when I had been good enough to give him a roof over his head at his time of need. I decided to nip into McDonald's for a cheeky burger on the way back. It tasted so amazing today.

I opened the front door and decided to go for the kill straight away. I asked Luca when he would be able to help me out with some rent as I was low on cash. He said his he would be paid soon and then he would not only contribute towards the rent but the grocery shopping too. He was very reassuring so I left it to that. I told him the dates that I would be out of town, in order to make sure that he would be in when I got back as there was only one set of keys. He said he would get an extra set cut which made sense. However, as he was still waiting for his wage to come through he asked me if he could borrow the equivalent to £100. This was really pushing it, but he swore that he would have the money ASAP! After all he was living with me. He was hardly going to do a runner. He mentioned that his employers would be sending him to Kuwait to cover some news stories. Coincidently he would be leaving the same day as me but would be returning two days before.

The days were passing like minutes and my time to head back home to the UK was right here.

I literally took an empty suitcase so I could load it up with as many things as possible to bring back to the UAE. It was a night flight and this time I had no one sitting next to me. What a relief!

All I wanted to do was get back to the UK as quickly as I could, so after dinner I slept through like a baby, and as planned I got to Manchester in what seemed like quick flash. I had pre-arranged with my aunt to pick me up and I knew she would bring my mum and grandmother. They would be equally eager to see me as I would be to see them. As I headed toward the sign that said, 'nothing to declare', I was stopped by security for a check. Just my luck! The good thing was there was barely anything in my suitcase which caused a bit of suspicion but I explained why to the best of my ability and eventually I was free to go.

As I went through the sliding doors I could see my little fan club waiting for me. All looking very emotional and ready to embrace me! It wasn't long before my water works opened and my eyes were filled with extra-large tears. We headed to the car and that was it non-stop chat all the way. I told them of my adventure so far and that I would shortly be working for a reputable media company. Everyone was so happy for me. One thing I did miss was home cooked food. My mouth was watering at the thought of my mum's pilau rice and my grandmother's chicken curry. What a great combination. I couldn't wait to see my little nephew too. No doubt he was not that little anymore. Every minute of this trip was going to be so precious because I had no idea of when I would return.

Everything was exactly how I had left it. I ran towards my favourite area of the sofa and lounged there for as long as I could. Even though it was not a mammoth flight it was still tiring. It did feel strange being back but I slotted in like I had not been away at all.

The food was spectacular as always. It was nice to have others looking after me rather than me having to do all the running around. Even though I was content with my new life I did miss these little things. I didn't want to do anything that evening. It was best for me to sleep off any tiredness so that I could tackle the rest of the week with ease. I also thought it wise to get as much done in the first couple of days so that I wasn't stressing for the rest of my stay.

I got up bright and early to raid my wardrobe and grab all I needed to. It didn't take long at all. To be honest other than clothing there wasn't much else that I required. It was easy enough to buy everything out there. The next thing on my to-do list was to contact all my model agencies to let them know that I had moved away, so please don't book me any work.

I walked over to my sister's house and there was my gorgeous nephew all smiles and ready to play with me.

After spending some priceless moments with him, it was time to get online and get those emails sent to the agencies. As I was writing out the emails a certain feeling of sadness was coming over me. I had been with these agencies for several years now and built a fantastic working relationship with them. It really did feel like an end of an era. Deep inside I was praying that I had made the right decision. It was a huge sacrifice as I was leaving my family, my full-on career and my life behind for something that still wasn't crystal clear. I had to remind myself how much I loved the way of life in Dubai, and more importantly, the heat which was a huge factor. All done just by the hit of a click! I was ticking off everything nicely on my list.

The only thing left was to say my goodbyes to everyone. I almost forgot I had one major task to complete and that was to get my certificates stamped. That's when I switched to panic mode. Still online I decided to check the opening times of the UAE consulate in London and try and work round when it would be best to go. Time sure was not on my side anymore. After careful consideration, I decided it was best to go to London on the day of my return to the UAE, even though my flight was from Manchester Airport. My flight wasn't till late evening, so I had enough time. I could leave for London very early in the morning, get all my documents authenticated and then head directly to the airport. I could get my aunt to take my suitcase in the car and I could meet everyone there. Not a bad idea! The only downside was that I would have to be running around like a headless chicken on that day. Not a problem as I was use to it! That was the finalised plan of action.

I could not believe that I was on my last night, time just flew by. It's not that I had a very heavy schedule during my stay or having a great deal to do, but time seems to slip away. I still hadn't seen my friends as yet, so decided to see them at where we initially met which was at the BBC Radio Lancashire, where we all worked. For me it had been about learning the art of radio and appreciating it as a medium. There was Amar, Shamim & Robina. I remember my first day there. I was like a rabbit in headlights. Shamim, a very strong intellectual and dynamic personality, and Amar & Robina were very laid back and chilled; all equally amazing inspiring individuals. I found Shamim a very direct person who never held back in what she said or did. I remember thinking to myself she's going to eat me alive, how will I survive here? In all respects, she showed me the ropes and I learnt a lot from her, not forgetting what a genuine kind, caring person she is. Needless to say, we became very good friends. It was paramount to see them before I left the country.

I managed to hitch a ride with my mum to Blackburn as the studios were located over there. It was only a fifteen minute-drive. I had this strange feeling inside as it was suddenly dawning on me that I would be leaving for good. We headed into the gallery where we had some of the best laughs over there. I was delighted and emotional for sure. We chatted for a short while and then reluctantly I said my goodbyes and then I left. I felt so happy that I had made the effort to see my friends. This strange feeling was getting stronger from within.

I needed to get a reasonably early night as I still had my trek to London to complete. My mum, sister, aunt & grandmother would be seeing me off at the airport. I wasn't looking forward to that at all. Everything was packed and I was ready to rock.

I left extremely early in the morning for London. It was a long and tedious journey taking a good four hours to get there. Just to add to it all, the weather was so miserable and wet. I had left my suitcase in the hallway for my aunt to collect and put into her car, just in case I was running late. I was travelling light which was a blessing. I used to hate coming into London for castings as all I used to see were tubes, stairs and a lot of miserable faces. The tube journey was short and sweet and I must have got there for about midday. The office looked as if it was packing up for lunch. I had to practically beg on all fours for them to take the documents and give them back to me as soon as possible. They tried every trick in the book to put me off and come back another time. How dare they! I kept saying I had a flight to catch the same day, and that I wouldn't be in the country. It was crucial to get them the same day. I must have put on a great show as eventually they gave in and reassured me that it would all be done within an hour. It was such hard work. Why couldn't they have just said that in the first place? Instead they enjoyed watching me sweat it out. All I could think was, 'Thank God!'

The hour passed swiftly and I had not moved from my seat. Finally, I had my documents in my hand. I kissed each and every one, making sure that they hadn't pulled a fast one on me, and that they had done the job properly. Yes, all stamped! I then ran out of there as fast as I could to get my train to Manchester Airport. It was the most peaceful journey ever. Everything was all done and dusted. I could relax.

As soon as I got off the train I called my aunt to see where they all were? Just as I had hung up, I could see everyone waiting in anticipation for me.

I ran towards them and hugged every single one. We only had a few more moments together before my departure. It was so hard seeing everyone look so upset at me leaving.

I did say that I would come as soon as I could, but I also said that I wanted everyone to come there and see me. Our family goodbyes were always prolonged, but this time I had no choice but to keep this short and sweet. We all had tears rolling down our faces. It was hugely painful. I hugged everyone for the last time. I told them how much I loved them and how much I would miss them. I had to leave before I missed my flight, I turned around and they were all crying. I gave a brave wave and headed to security. At that moment, I felt my life just flash by me. I pulled myself together, went through security then headed for the gate. My head was full of thoughts and I was lost in my own world. I was woken up by the screeching sound of an elderly lady telling us all that we would start boarding now. It was a busy flight but as long as I had a window seat I was happy. I did and I was very content.

We reached Dubai twenty minutes before our scheduled time. I got a taxi and headed home. When I got there, both Luca and Ethan were asleep. I was getting annoyed because it felt like Ethan was spending an awful lot of time at my so called house. The place looked so messy. I was not impressed at all. I calmly put my luggage down and then switched the television on with the volume on high. That seemed to work. They reluctantly got up. I asked Ethan how work was and if he was going to be working that day. He said he had a late shift. Luca also had work that day. I was so relieved to hear this.

I told him that I got all my documents stamped. He seemed surprised that I was so on the case. He also said that my visa would be delayed as it needed to be approved by several departments before it would actually reach me. He also said that I would need to give £400 more because he got mixed up with the cost of fees. I was livid at that point, my blood was boiling! I argued that I had already given a vast amount of money and there still was no sign of my visa! What kind of company was this? Why was I being messed around? It wasn't something I wanted to hear on my return. Again, he seemed to have this way of calming me down, he assured me that it would all be sorted out soon. I needed to work. It was becoming a huge worry. He mentioned that he had a project coming in for which they would be requiring models, singers, presenters, fashion designers, and I was to help him recruit this creative team. Once the project was in full swing, I would be paid for my time. By then my visa would have been sorted out, I would be comfortable and have plenty of work. Again, I felt more assured. For the first time ever, Luca had bought some bread and cheese, we all had breakfast together and then the two headed out.

I paid the extra £400 to Luca. I didn't want it hanging over me. I wanted to sleep for a few hours more, then get up and cook dinner early. I messaged my sister to tell her I'd arrived in Dubai safe and sound.

I was knocked out for a good while. I made the call to the grocery shop and they delivered efficiently as always. There was a little drawer near the cooker that housed matchsticks and lighters to use for when I was cooking. I put my hand in but couldn't feel anything, so I pushed my hand in further. I felt some paper on the match box and pulled it towards me. There were two receipts stuck together which was from the fast food place that I normally order from. The strange thing was that it was dated the day that I had left for the UK, and the time was for 6pm the same evening. How could that be? Neither of us had been home. I was travelling to the UK and Luca to Kuwait. The other receipt was for the exact same amount, two meals dated for the following day at the same time in the evening. This was really baffling. There was no one else who had the keys. How could this be? Maybe Luca was lying to me and that he didn't go anywhere. Why would he lie to me?

I needed to get to the bottom of this as it was so confusing and very frustrating. All I kept thing was why did Luca lie to me? That night when Luca strolled in I said that I had found two receipts in the drawer and they were dated for the days we weren't even in the country. How was that possible? He denied any knowledge of them as he was in Kuwait. This was really making my head hurt! It did not make any sense from any direction. In the end, I gave up on trying to piece it together. Little did I know this was a very small sign of what was to come!

I needed to check my emails to see if any more agencies had been in touch or if there were any exciting opportunities for me, so I went to my local. As always it was busy, but I found a nice little spot. I was very happy to see that I had received lots of replies from agencies etc. There was one particular reply that was of great interest to me. An events company were launching their business and wanted me to come up with a concept for a commercial to showcase all the services they provided as an organisation. It wasn't paying great but who was I to argue with that? Something was better than nothing. It was a great opportunity to showcase my skills in marketing. At least I had something to get my teeth into. The deadline was ASAP. I always enjoyed working to short deadlines. A couple of other agencies had registered me on their database and wanted me to attend castings straight away.

The next few days were very busy with about four castings a day.

It was hard work going to see potential clients, putting on my best face and dripping in the heat. The temperature was soaring thick and fast. It just made the running around much more difficult. After all the castings were covered I worked very hard on the commercial. I think out of the box and like to be innovative. I came up with a winning idea.

The idea was that it was filmed in a large white room. All you would see was a white table at the far end with a funky looking clear jug and an empty glass on it. The jug would be half full of water with a few ice cubes in it. The camera then sees a model initially out of focus walking like she's on the catwalk towards the table; you only have a back view of the model and all you hear is the sound of her stiletto heels. As she gets closer to the table she becomes more in focus, she picks up the jug and fills her glass of water and takes a long sip before putting the glass back down. She begins to walk to where she started, as she gets closer to the camera she becomes less in focus, and the glass on the table becomes more in focus as it's moving side to side and falls. The water shoots out of the glass and then the ice cubes begin to crack, and inside each ice cube you get a model advertising all the different services that the event company offers, i.e. a model in one cube, a singer in another, a designer in another and so on. It was a very satisfying job and I really did prove my worth.

There was one particular email that had me in shock but a good kind of shock. One of my very dear celebrity friends from London, Shahin Badar, was going to come to Dubai to see me. I couldn't believe it. She's an amazing international singer with a very soulful voice who has worked with some of the biggest bands ever including The Prodigy who I totally love. I had always been a huge fan of hers and when the opportunity came up to interview her for the BBC, I embraced it! We got on so well like a house on fire! Funny enough, I discovered her clothing designer was my mum's first cousin. Such a small world! We had become very good friends and kept in touch. We always met when I went to London. This was such great news. I emailed her back to say that I couldn't wait to see her. She would be the coming in the next few weeks.

CHAPTER 9

The weeks were passing by and I was beginning to feel a bit burnt out with all the running around. Luca had asked me to put an advertisement in the Gulf News advertising for all types of entertainers for a pilot TV show that would be filmed in a proper studio in a few weeks. I got onto it straight away. My phone was like a hotline number, with endless calls from people desperately wanting to make it in the entertainment industry. Models, singers, actors, presenters, you name it. All different nationalities, all very hungry for success! I was briefed by Luca to take all their details and tell them we would be in touch very soon. This would be done at one mass casting where everyone would be invited to showcase their talent. The turnout was phenomenal.

Then one day, something really strange happened which to this day does not make any sense to me. Luca said that we were invited to a game show where we needed some people. We would have to make a team of these people and they would be participating in challenges live on air. He would put the team together from all the interest I had from the adverts which he did. We turned up to this event and it was buzzing. A fantastic atmosphere! I had no idea with what was going on because everything was in Arabic. The participants had to do various challenges and whichever team completed the most challenges, they would be the winners and receive money as a reward. It so turned out that our team ended up winning. They announced the winners and Luca said I should go up and receive the cash from the host. I didn't understand why it had to be me, why not him? I couldn't speak the language, I couldn't converse with them and tell them of my experience, so why me? I hadn't even taken part!

Anyway, like an idiot I went on live television where millions were watching me take the cash. Luca snatched it out of my hands before I could even hand it over to him. He told the contestants that he would share the money amongst them all. I understood this as some of the contestants spoke English and then he muttered something in Arabic. From what I could see, the contestants had their hands out waiting for their reward, but instead Luca talked to them and they nodded their heads in agreement, then he put the money away in his pocket and that was that!

Having had more great response from agencies, I decided to do a schedule for myself which would entail me meeting all the agents in a short space of time. Little bits and pieces were coming in which was positive, however they sure took their time in paying up.

Luca said he had a friend who was a fashion designer and that I should call him to arrange a meet up so that's exactly what I did.

His name was Yaroob, originally of Iraqi origin but residing in Sharjah. He seemed quite pleasant and passionate about his work. We arranged to meet at a mall in Sharjah. He looked very young and like he had starved himself. He was very skinny. He said he was working on his next collection. I used that as a cue to say that I would be more than happy to model for him. It seemed quite productive so far but then I had to make a move as I had to go agency trekking. He said he was free and would be more than happy to accompany me on my missions. I didn't mind him coming except he became a bit of a cling on, and would expect me to pay for his lunch and dinner especially on longer days. I didn't mind doing it here and there, but every meal was a bit too much. I was really beginning to feel used. I needed to buckle up and start taking charge. After all I was in control of my own life! I didn't see or hear of Yaroob for a while.

Luca needed another reminder about the fact that he had borrowed some money from me. I very politely asked him for my money, and all I got back was that he was still waiting for his wage. Not good enough. I was at the point where my funds were extremely low. It was time for me to do the most dreaded thing, to ask my brother for some money. It was not my style but things were getting to the point of desperation as I was lagging behind with the rent and needed to cover two months, as well as needing some money to live on. I had juiced out my credit cards thanks to Luca and his demands for money here and there. It all mounted up to a substantial amount. I felt so ashamed to even think about asking my family. I had no choice so I called up my brother. I hadn't spoken to him in ages which made me feel worse. The time I did call him I needed a favour, but then, that's what families are there for. I would pay him back as soon as I got paid. It was just a short-term loan.

It was so nice to hear my brother's voice. We talked for quite some time. It was a great catch up until I had to ask that horrid question. I just came out with it assuring him that my visa would be sorted ASAP and that I would pay him back as soon as the money started coming in. I said I would never have asked if I wasn't in such a desperate situation. My brother very kindly agreed to send me £2000 via Western Union as that was the only way to get money to me quickly. Mission accomplished. What a relief that was. I would have been so screwed had he not been able to help me out. I was eternally grateful.

I so enjoyed making that call to the landlord to come and pick up the rent.

There was quite a healthy number of talented people interested in working with us on Luca's project, so that evening he dragged me to the Al Ghurair centre to meet a few of them face to face. I sat there like a lemon not having any idea what they were talking about. Occasionally I would get a look from the attendees. They would break into a bit of a smile and then carry on talking to Luca. He used me and my expertise to sell himself to people because of the fact I was from the UK and I was established to a high level in my field. That gave people a vote of confidence in what he was saying. I hated being dragged to these meetings. I really did not see the point of my presence there. Unfortunately for me, these meetings were taking place far too often. We had built up a huge network of people. He was also speaking to hotels like Claridge Dubai and other independent businesses that were happy to part with their money for this and upcoming projects. This gave me the vote of confidence that something good was developing. The next step was to do a pilot shoot of the concept for this lifestyle television show. Luca was very confident with this project as he claimed to know a lot of locals. It's the locals that call the shots and have a lot say. Anything is possible if you have a local on your side.

I left early from the meeting. It had been quite an eventful day. I just wanted to rest up. Quite a few hours later Luca walked in beaming away. He was very excited about the project. Everything seemed to be going the way he had planned. I was feeling a little irritated because my visa still had not come so I asked Luca when it would be sorted. There had been a ridiculous amount of time and money spent. This time I went for it and argued my case. All he kept saying was, 'do you not trust me'? It was almost like he was using reverse psychology. Still very upset and angry I went to bed.

I got up at around 11am. I slept reasonably well considering there was so much going on in my mind. I headed towards the bathroom to brush my teeth; I picked up my toothbrush case which had my toothbrush in it. I was about to put it in my mouth until I saw the most disgusting thing sitting on my toothbrush. I was in complete shock! It was a piece of human faeces. I was heaving so badly that I vomited violently all over the floor. Who the hell had done this vile thing? Only I and Luca had the keys. It was not possible for anyone to have come into the apartment, unless they were thieves, and if they *did*, they would have taken things and not committed such as disgraceful act. Did I really see it? Was it in my imagination? I felt like I was going mad.

That evening when Luca came in, I lashed out on him because realistically it could only have been him, but he completely denied it and swore blind he was not the type of person to do anything like that, and why would he do it to me? He had a point, but whom else could it have been? It was all very unsettling and very discomforting. To add fuel to the whole situation he said that Ethan had lost his job and that he would be living with us. I hit the bloody roof. How dare he invite someone else to live in my house when he wasn't even contributing towards anything? He could at least have had the decency to ask. I mean, was my home some kind of open house for people? This was really taking the biscuit and hugely disrespectful for me.

It all blew up into a huge argument. It was intolerable, so I told him to get out of my home, *now*! He sheepishly took his man bag and slammed the door right behind him. I felt a sense of huge relief. I didn't need this. I had been taken advantage of. It was about time I had said my piece. Enough was enough! I started to unwind properly and made myself a strong cup of tea. I couldn't be bothered to run out and grab a real cuppa from my local. It felt nice to have the place to myself. I was hoping I would never see that ungrateful and unappreciative person again.

A few hours on and there was a knock at the door. Guess who? Luca and Ethan! Why? He was apologetic and had brought some dinner as peace offering. That wasn't good enough. He was very calm and said that this arrangement would only be a short-term thing. Ethan was being abnormally nice and again they both talked me out of my decision. I was such a soft touch. Luca also said that his family was going to send some money over and that he would be giving some of it to me. He said that he would have to go to a bank in Sharjah to get it. Ethan suggested we should all go for the ride and maybe have dinner in the mall.

Everyone one was up early. For once I didn't have to make breakfast or clear the dishes. I was being waited on for a refreshing change. They were both trying to be on their best behaviour because in effect they had a lot to lose.

I asked Ethan what happened regarding his job situation and he said that his contract had come to an end. He didn't want to renew it as he wanted to relocate to London. He also wanted to head back to Brazil to see his family before his move.

It was a calm and relaxed day and we decided to get ready to go to Sharjah. The cheapest and quickest way to get there was to stand in an area just off Nasser Square from where you can hitch a ride.

You had to share a car with strangers but it wasn't too bad as there were three of us already so there would only be room for two more people. This was all done the unofficial way but it was exciting and cheap! The traffic was crawling and it was awfully hot in the car. We got dropped off very close to the mall where the bank was. I waited outside the bank whilst the two of them went in. It seemed to take forever. They came out about fifty minutes later and said that it hadn't come through and that there were some technical errors. Luca said he would call his family to see why the transaction never happened. More empty reassurances. I was surely more disappointed than the both of them put together. We headed towards the food court for dinner and guess who paid? Me of course! It was a good time to tell them that my friend Shahin was coming to London the following day and that I was going to go to the airport to meet her and will be spending quality time with her. I so needed this. Her visit was a true blessing for me indeed!

CHAPTER 10

Just a few more hours, and I would be seeing a familiar face. I could not sleep. My head was filled with a mixture of thoughts which made it impossible for me to relax.

I must have had just a couple of hours of sleep which clearly was not enough when I saw myself in the mirror. I had bags down to my ankles. I was beginning to look a bit gaunt and basically out of it. I felt much fresher after a shower. The others were sleeping and so I left a post-it on the fridge to tell them to make sure everything was clean and tidy by the time I got back as I didn't want Shahin to see my place looking messy. I know how particular she is about these things. Rightfully so! I am the same. I was all ready and early, as usual. I was eagerly waiting to see her come through the doors and suddenly there she was, looking radiant as always. Her warm smile and positive aura seemed to bring me round to the feeling of normality again. Despite the fact I had been feeling very abnormal! We greeted each other with a nice warm hug and headed out to get a taxi, happily chatting all the way as we hadn't seen each other for a very long time. There was so much to catch up on.

It was decided that I would drop her off at the hotel and let her freshen up. I would head home and we would meet later in the day. She checked in all comfortably then I headed home. Of course, no cleaning had been done because the two lazy unappreciative people were too busy sleeping. I got them up and tidied up the place up myself. I was a complete mug! By the time everything was in shape I got a call from Shahin to say that she would be arriving soon. I quickly showered again as it was becoming hotter by the minute and I was sweating like crazy after the quick cleaning spree. I didn't mind, it was just an inconvenience to keep showering every few minutes.

I was going to meet Shahin just a short walk away from the apartment. She was there already. We had just walked a few yards when somebody shouted her name really loudly as they had recognised her. We strolled back to mine at a good chilled out pace. I was hoping Ethan and Luca would make themselves scarce so that I could have peace and quality time with my friend. Unfortunately, they were too shameless to leave. I introduced them to her. Thankfully they seemed to be on their best behaviour. It was me that wasn't feeling very comfortable. I was glad that she felt comfortable and that they were chatting to her respectfully.

I had missed hearing her sing and so asked her to sing a few lines. She sang so beautifully. It gave me goose pimples. She is blessed with such an amazing talent. I felt very proud of her.

It was fast approaching lunch time and I was going to cook a very simple dish. Sardines with chilli and lemon! It was so quick and easy but had the ultimate taste. I heated the oil in a wok, threw in some onions and garlic. Cooked it for a little while then added the sardines and red chilli powder. Once it was fully cooked I squeezed fresh lemon onto it before serving. It was delicious with the Lebanese bread. Everybody thoroughly enjoyed it. I was very impressed with myself. The rest of the evening we spent chatting and chilling then Luca randomly suggested that he knew a poet and it would be great for Shahin to meet him as he would really appreciate her vocals for his poetry. He was going to confirm a time and place with the poet for the following day. It was getting late as it had hit the early hours of the morning. I got a cab sorted for Shahin and made sure she was comfortable getting back to her hotel.

So as planned the following day we all met with the poet in a café not too far away from the apartment. He was indeed very talented with the way he used his words in his work. Very deep and philosophical! I felt that Luca and Ethan were going out of their way to please Shahin to make a good impression because of who she was rather than for the sincerity. I felt that very slowly, they were unveiling their true colours. The evening ended pleasantly and for the rest of Shahin's stay we chilled out, went to nice cafes and restaurants, had some really nice walks and enjoyed some quality time without the cling-ons. She had lots of television and magazine interviews and I accompanied her. It was a great way for me to meet people in the media. I left my contact details everywhere we went just in case anyone ever required my services. Unfortunately, her stay had come to an end. I just wished she could have stayed on longer. I felt very sad leaving her at the airport, as did she.

Still feeling sad about my friend leaving, Ethan said he was going to treat us all for dinner in the evening. I almost fell off the sofa in shock. This was a one off which I didn't want to miss. At the same time, I felt maybe there was a motive for his actions. I was becoming very wary of them both. Still, a free dinner was not the worst thing in the world. One by one we were getting ready for our big night out.

We were going to a restaurant called 'The Golden Fork' which had a good selection of seafood and Arabic food. Not to forget their choice of milkshakes. It was only a short walk away.

I really loved the strolls in the evening as the air was so sweet and soothing. The restaurant had a lovely vibe and I was starving. I wanted everything off the menu.

We ordered a mezze which was huge and so filling. I was surprised at how quickly I got full up. I was making most of the evening and enjoying myself until Ethan started to talk about how amazingly good looking he is and that people stop him in the street to check him out. I remember thinking, 'get a life mate!' He basically described himself as God's gift to humanity. I almost choked on the fruit that I was nibbling at. He then had the audacity to turn to me and say that I was very average and that he was surprised I was a model and that when he becomes a model no-one would ever even look at me let alone book me. I was upset and furious! Normally I wouldn't be affected by any of this kind of talk but for some reason I was feeling much more vulnerable. I defended myself to the best of my ability in a dignified way but there was no stopping him. He went on and on and Luca sat there with a smirk on his face which wound me up more. I had given these people a roof over their head, fed them, given them money and this was how I was repaid? Insult after insult.

I felt so upset that I walked out of the restaurant and headed home. My feelings were really hurt. Why was I feeling so weak? I was normally a very strong and confident person. It was so out of character for me. I got home and I don't know what came over me but I did something very childish and again totally out of character. I hid in my wardrobe that had a shutter style door and waited for them to come back. About twenty minutes later, I heard the sound of rummaging keys. Then the door opened with both Ethan and Luca laughing as they came in. The light came on and I could see them scuttle around the room saying, 'is he here?' Then the other said 'no its all clear.' They continued with more insults at me including the fact that I was financially sorted so why should they contribute towards rent. I was fuming! How dare they! Then I witnessed the most unexpected thing. They both started to strip and walk towards my bed. I couldn't contain myself anymore. I jumped out of the cupboard and they jumped out of their skins. Their faces were worth a picture as they were so shocked and horrified. I shouted at them for disrespecting me and then ran out of the apartment.

I could not make head or tail of the situation. I needed some air to clear my head. I walked for a good half an hour then headed back. It was all calm and quiet. They were both asleep. I slipped into my night clothes and tried to sleep with a much stressed out mind.

It was more than awkward in the morning. I didn't say a word and left to go out. I had a meeting with a magazine who wanted to feature me in their forthcoming issue. It was more of an interview of me and my career.

They were interested in what had brought me to Dubai and how the fashion industry was different to the UK and so forth. The lady that interviewed me was a real gem and so hospitable and professional at her job. She asked me all the right questions and was portraying me in a very positive light. I left feeling on a real high.

My phone rang and it was a local number calling me. I picked up wondering who it could be. My expression changed from anxious to happy. I had just been booked to do some catwalk shows for a jeans company called 'Newport' who is the equivalent to Levi's. Every cloud indeed has a silver lining. It had really paid off in more ways than one going to the meetings with Shahin as one of the companies had kept my details and remembered what I did for a living and so booked me to do a whole day of shows. My work really was my biggest passion and the key to my happiness.

By the time I got home my focus was on my productive day and not of the events that took place the previous evening. I walked in to find Ethan and Luca doing some paper work. A date had been set for all the talented people that I had recruited to meet for an official get together at the Claridges hotel. It was all happening. At the meeting, everyone would have to showcase their talents in front of everyone. My job would be to do a routine on the catwalk and then get the models to copy it. I would also have to start allocating roles to the rest of the recruits. Nothing was said about yesterday. To be honest I didn't want to waste my energy on the negativity. I wanted to focus on all the positive things that were happening. We had two days to get everything in order to pull this project together as at the meeting we would be briefing everyone on the plan for the pilot shoot and how the day would be structured, i.e. location, what to bring etc. I also had my catwalk shows to look forward to which were taking place a day after the big thrash out meeting. Then Ethan said the magic words that brought music to my ears. He was leaving Dubai once and for all. His plan was to go to Brazil first then head to London. I really thought I would never live to see the day. He was going to be leaving the day after the meeting. I was ecstatic. One down, one to go!

There was a lot to do for the meeting as there needed to be some form of structure. It needed to be professional. It's either everything or nothing with me. That's the way I have always worked. I let Luca do most of the prep work as I had put in a lot of time and effort previously.

It was quite straight forward. Ethan was more than eager to help a lending hand to Luca. All I could think of was that after the briefing day there would be more space in my apartment. I was literally counting down the hours.

Lord behold, the day I was waiting for had arrived. Ethan had done all his packing the night before. All day was spent sorting the schedule for the meeting and having a register of who was attending. The ones that spoke English had my number to call should any queries arise. I ordered some food in as we were so rushed off our feet. I didn't mind paying because I was feeling very content. We knocked down the food quickly and headed to the venue. I was very quiet on the way. I didn't feel like I wanted to have any meaningless conversations with either of them.

It was a full house. Thankfully the hotel had kindly given us a good size room to house everyone for that evening. They even threw in some refreshments. That's Middle Eastern hospitality for you. Everyone on the list had showed up. I had got to know some of them and they were really nice people. Some looked quite roughed up and not very approachable. I left them for Luca to deal with because they didn't speak much English either. I started the evening by welcoming everyone and thanking them for attending. Luca took over and started with the briefing. He explained that the turnaround was quick. He had joined forces with a local woman called Fatimah who was interested in coming on board with this venture. This meant we had more access to a lot more resources and much more flexibility in what we wanted to achieve. We would be filming a pilot in a studio in Ajman the following week. It would be a whole day job so everyone needed to be available and if not they needed to speak up now. Amazingly everyone was available.

It was refreshing to see how serious everyone was taking this. Clearly, they had a lot of passion and dedication. It was quite a fun evening and I enjoyed doing my walk and helping some of the models to better their walk and build their confidence. All in all, it was a hugely successful evening. Everyone went out of the room with big smiles on their faces even the miserable ones!

The best part of the evening was yet to come: Ethan's exit! As we got closer to home, I was feeling quite parched and so went to the coffee shop whilst the other two headed home. I got myself a double dose of tea. It was well deserved. After finishing my second cup I headed to the apartment where Ethan had gathered his belongings ready to leave.

I was civil and said goodbye. Luca was very sad that Ethan was leaving so he walked him to his taxi. I felt I could breathe better. It was Luca's turn next. That was my ultimate wish.

Luca returned and we didn't exchange much in conversation. I just wanted my bed and that's exactly what I got. It was the end of another full-on day.

I was getting more castings but direct work was becoming a bit slow. It was a cause for concern because funds were low once again. I was up bright and early as I had a casting to go to. I grabbed my portfolios and as I was leaving, Luca said that he had lined up a casting for me too. It was a local man looking for a model to front his business. When I asked what kind of business he had he just said he specialised in menswear and wanted a good model to front his campaign. He said it was paying well. I took the client's number. He was called Khalid. I decided that I would call him in a few days once I had completed my catwalk shows as that way I could focus properly on it.

Another productive day! The photographer loved the versatility in my portfolio and said I had a very strong editorial look. It would now be the decision of the client which meant waiting, waiting and waiting some more. It's good to put it all behind you once the casting has taken place, much better not to think about it. If you get the job, that's a bonus. If not, it's a good way to create awareness of one's existence.

I was feeling quite upbeat until I walked into my home to see that Luca had invited one of the models for tea. Again, he did not have the courtesy to ask me. This particular model didn't have a friendly face. He was so tall and hugely built and quite intimidating. All I learnt was that he was Egyptian, nothing else. He could speak some broken English but only spoke in Arabic to Luca which was very rude. I was feeling very uncomfortable and so decided to go and have a fix of tea at the café. Whilst in the café I made a list of the things I would need to take for the shows. I like to be organised even though the client was providing everything. It's always good to be prepared and take various coloured belts, shoes, hairspray, a basic makeup kit and different coloured underwear. You just never know!

CHAPTER 11

Another blissful morning! The sun was shining like a precious jewel. My bag was packed for work. The great thing was there were rarely early starts because life began much later in Dubai. I could always get a lie in which really helped because I always looked really fresh and perked up, even though it may not have been the case from within.

It had come to the point where I didn't make any effort with Luca. I only spoke when I had to. That was more than enough as far as I was concerned. He had it all on a plate and had shown no respect or appreciation. Knowing full well that I didn't really want him around anymore, he remained shameless and stayed on.

I put on my jeans and t-shirt. I kept the look very simple because today I would be taking my clothes on and off for work, strange though it sounds. I had mastered the art of taking my clothes off and getting dressed into a full new outfit in just twenty-five seconds. That's quite a skill! It gets crazy behind the scenes of a fashion show even though all the models look so cool calm and collected whilst on the catwalk. I put on my sunglasses, grabbed my bag and headed out.

As I got close to Nasser square where the taxi stand was, I realised that I didn't have my mobile phone with me after having a good rummage in my bag. I had a short panic attack then I remembered that I had left it on the table next to my coffee mug. I always put it there once I turned off the alarm. I didn't need it and it wasn't as if it wouldn't be there when I got back!

The shows were held outdoors near a department store. When I got there the stage was being constructed. It was beginning to take shape nicely. I had a good idea of where we would be walking and where we would need to pose. All the models were backstage in the marquee which was also constructed especially for the show. It sure was stuffy in there with all the body heat and the fact that it was roasting outside. There was a fitter allocated between two models that would help us get dressed. The briefing was short and sweet. Before going into hair and make-up we had to do a rehearsal of the whole show to get a clearer idea of the running order. It was very straight forward as we had a T shaped catwalk which is what I consider to be a normal catwalk. I have walked on some very unusual and more complex stages. As soon as I am on stage I switch into model mode. The pout and mean and moody look comes out and I do my thing. I love it! After a quick run through it was time the get the face painted. There were only forty minutes left before show time and so the hair and makeup artists were working like the clappers. I really liked my outfits because they were so casual and comfortable. The choreographer seemed quite relaxed as he took us to our positions. I was first on and even though I have walked the runway many a times I always get butterflies in my stomach and they were doing some serious somersaults in there! The music kicked in, I waited for the beat and then went out. The amusing thing was as soon as I took a few strides, the makeup started to melt because of the intense heat. Like a professional I carried on and finished my routine. As soon as I got back stage the makeup artists were guarded with their weapons to sort the melting faces out. I really enjoyed doing the shows. It didn't for a minute feel like I was working. It was short and sweet. It was kind of the clients to let us all keep our jeans too which is very rare as these days the clients hold onto every piece of their garment like gold dust. I left feeling on a great level.

I got home and threw my bag on the bed. I went into the fridge to get a nice cold can of coke. I sat down on the sofa and put it on the table. The coffee mug had been cleared by Luca. I then remembered having left my phone on the table except it wasn't there. I searched high and low and could not find it. I emptied out my bag just in case it had slipped into the side somewhere, but nothing. I checked inside the wardrobes and did a thorough check everywhere but it wasn't to be seen. I was 100% sure that I had left it on the table. Luca wasn't at home. Maybe he had borrowed it for some reason. I began to panic because I had all my contacts on there and it was a new phone. I was really upset. How would I contact anyone now or them contact me? I frantically carried on with my search with the hope that it would show up. I heard the door open and Luca came in. I asked him if he had seen my phone. He said 'no' without any hesitation. I said that I had left it on the table before leaving for work, so how could it magically disappear? Nothing was making sense. I knew I had left it on the table. I was so tired too. Then Luca said that he would send a message to my phone saying that if anyone has found the phone to contact him. But I didn't take it with me! I tried to keep calm and not stress and keep that glimmer of hope of it returning to me.

The next day Luca said he received a text message saying that my phone had been found and the person that found it would arrange a meeting place for me to pick it up. I gave a sigh of relief. I waited all day but nothing, no contact from this mystery person that claimed to have found my phone.

I said to Luca to call that person or at least let me speak to them, he then changed his story and said that no one was coming and that it wasn't found!

He had contradicted himself evidently and was messing with my head again. The question was, where did my phone get to? Did he sell it? I was finally beginning to realise that he was testing me to see how much I trusted him and how far he could push it with me. It turned out that I had a lot of trust in him because I trusted everyone. Was I wrongly accusing him? Maybe it fell out of my bag at some point. Had that been the case I would have surely got it back as Dubai is notorious for being safe from these things. If someone did find my phone they wouldn't dare keep it as the chance of them being deported for theft is way too high. I didn't know what to think anymore so I decided to call the police to report it just in case.

I really wasn't feeling myself. My stress levels were hitting the roof. I was always on edge. Luca however was always a bit too calm and very blasé about everything which was a cause for concern deep down.

Fortunately, I had another contract phone from UK. It was still frustrating as I had lost all my numbers from Dubai! I would have to get that phone unlocked and report my other phone missing to the network provider too so that they would issue me with another SIM card that I could then use in this phone which meant another trip to Etisalat, the network provider. It was going to be a mission but it needed to be done sooner rather than later as otherwise I would be without contact with the outside world.

It all got sorted much more efficiently than I had envisaged, almost like a miracle. With my head being cluttered with so much tension I had completely forgotten about my visa situation. I checked the date of my standard visa that I had on my passport and to my horror I only had a week left on it before it would expire. Luca was not at home so I called him up to ask him about my visa. He very casually said that my visa didn't go through for whatever reason but not to worry because he knew a local woman who would happily sort it out! I would be meeting her at the pilot shoot so that would confirm everything. I naturally flipped at this point and told him that I had invested all that money into it and I wanted it back because my funds were extremely low. He said he was sorry but that would not be possible as it was non-refundable. I couldn't believe my luck as in total I had lost well over £3000. He calmed me down with great difficulty and again reassured me that this local lady was a good friend who had all the right contacts.

It came to the stage where I didn't know who to believe or what to believe. In a way, I felt that I had no choice but take his word for it. I tried to enjoy that bit of time at home whilst Luca was out. I was flicking through my phone and completely restless.

I switched the television on and my favourite programme was on but I just wasn't in the mood. One of the characters Khalid was in a lot of trouble and there was a lot of drama going on. I needed to watch something happy and cheerful however randomly it reminded me of the guy Luca had mentioned, the client who was also called Khalid that was interested in booking me for his campaign. I didn't have his number anymore as I had lost my phone with all my contacts so I called Luca to get his number. He didn't pick up the phone so I tried several times until eventually he picked up asking me what the emergency was? I briefly explained and he said that he would text the number straight away. He never kept to his word so this would be a little test.

To my disbelief a text message followed shortly after I put the phone down. This was a shock to my system! I didn't have much planned that evening so decided to be constructive by giving Khalid a call and arranging a meeting. We were going to meet at the Al Ghurair centre as it had some nice coffee shops and wasn't too far to walk. I nipped out to get some food as I needed some fresh air to cool down. It was a day for burger and chips. It's strange how I always opted for this kind of food when stressed. It gave me a short fix of comfort. I ate it quickly in the restaurant as I needed to get ready for my meeting.

I got home and ran into the shower. It didn't take me long to get dressed. This time I made sure the phone was in my bag. I checked several times. I would have been totally screwed if I lost this phone. That was not going to happen!

It was quiet in the café and I really longed for an iced coffee with lots of cream on it but I thought it would be rude to start drinking on my own so I waited. Khalid called me which was a good thing as I didn't have a clue what he looked like. I knew he would be wearing the dishdash but everyone did so that wasn't much of a giveaway. He located me after giving him a huge wave. He was well groomed and in his late forties. He seemed very pleased to see me and kept smiling. I did feel uncomfortable but didn't show it as he was a potential client. He talked very passionately about his clothing business and that it would be great for me to be the face of his latest collection. He then asked what I wanted to drink and I went straight in for the kill with my creamy calorific frappucino.

From what I gathered he was a well to do guy and obviously money was no object which was consoling as that would mean that I would get paid well without having to put up a fight for it.

I was quite excited and looking forward to the campaign. We chatted for quite a while longer and then Khalid suggested that we should go to his showroom to check out some of his clothes and maybe try a few samples on.

I wasn't in any real rush so decided to go. We headed towards the car park. He had a beautiful car. It was a black sleek Lamborghini. I dread to think the value of it. He opened my door and I got in. The interiors were stunning in red leather. It was like stepping into another world. He was very level headed and seemed very relaxed talking to me. As he was driving he kept looking over to me which was very discomforting. Then as if from nowhere his hand touched my knee! I jumped a little due to the shock then his hand was sliding up my leg and I told him to take his hand off whilst trying to keep calm. He didn't listen so I started to shout, telling him to take his bloody hand off my leg. He gripped my leg tighter and I started to scream at the top of my lungs. We were in a very quiet residential area and thankfully at this point the car was stationary. I tried to open the door but it was locked. My heart was skipping many beats. I could not believe what was happening.

I forcefully tried opening the door again and still no movement. I carried on shouting and he began to shout too saying he had paid Luca the equivalent of £3000 for me to spend time with him, of course I had no idea about and that he would not be paying the remaining of £2000 which was the remaining payment. I was livid and feeling so disgusted. He finally clicked the locks of the car door open and I got myself out of the car as soon as I could whilst he continued to hail abuse at me in English and Arabic.

It was one shock after another. I couldn't take it! The realisation of the situation was becoming more apparent. That evil person Luca had pimped me out like a prostitute in order to get a few quid for himself. How self-centred and greedy can you get? That was the lowest act I had ever experienced. I was not going to let this one drop at any cost! I had made up my mind that I wanted Luca out. He was a user and only cared for himself. No normal human being would act in this way.

I was beginning to feel very alone and isolated from normality. Instead I was in the midst of extreme negative surrealism. I was all fired up and ready to explode on Luca.

Luckily for him he wasn't home when I reached there. I snuggled up on the sofa with a blanket and tried to divert my attention to anything else but it was proving very difficult.

Eventually Luca came home. I had managed to get a bit of sleep and was a bit calmer. I thought it would be best to handle this situation calmly. I told him how I had been treated by Khalid and that I knew of his disgusting plan about selling me off.

Of course, as always, he denied it saying that he was taking an advance commission for the shoot I was going to be booked for and that he was taking his cut for getting me the gig. I mean please, really! I had had enough and wasn't going to hold back. So, without even taking a breath I let loose and said everything that I had kept inside for such a long time, including the fact that he was ungrateful, money grabbing, and such a greedy person who only thought about himself, not to forget the fact that he was living off me. I saved the best bit till last and told him that I wanted him out and not to ever contact me again.

The response was greater than what I imagined. He said that he would be leaving Dubai for good to go back to Lebanon shortly after the pilot shoot and that it would be his local friend that would take over the project. He also said that he wanted to make sure my visa was sorted. I bit back and said that he hadn't proved himself as a friend so far, so why did he now care whether I got my visa sorted or not? He said he did appreciate all that I did and that I was a great loyal friend. My anger was just increasing but I needed to contain myself. 'Just think of the positive', I kept saying to myself. He would be gone soon enough.

Being in this situation was teaching me a lot. I felt I was being stripped of my nice and kind nature in order to survive the sharks of the world. There was nothing else that I could do other than wait for his exit and celebrate that. It was at times like this where I dearly missed my family. I had lately been so wrapped up in myself that I hadn't even called anyone to see if they were ok. It was not intentional of course. I just needed things to get back to normal and to get rid of the negativity that was blanketing my life at present. Being positive and patient was a strong trait of mine and no matter how bad or difficult the situation, it was important to continue to think like that. As they say, all good things come to those who wait. That's what I needed to do. Just hang on a little longer. Everything would be fine?

CHAPTER 12

The day of the pilot shoot finally arrived. I was keeping it completely professional with Luca now. I didn't have the time or energy for anything more. I had done more than my fair share without doubt. It was going to be the longest day ever. The studio was based in Ajman which meant a bit of travelling. We would have to allow at least an hour to get there. The main thing was that the project was moving forward and hopefully my visa would be sorted soon because it was a matter of days before it would run out.

We got a taxi to Ajman. I refused to pay and so Luca had to dig deep in his pockets to cough up. It was only fair. An hour's journey of silence felt like a life time. The views were nice and proved to be a great distraction. It was my first visit to Ajman and it was quite different to Dubai in the sense that it wasn't as crazy in terms of the full-on traffic. There weren't too many crowds either. It seemed quite like a sleepy town in comparison to the wild vibe of Dubai. The studio was situated even further away from civilization. From outside it was not very pleasing to the eye. However inside was a completely different story! High ceilings, masses of space, lots of lights, cameras, but not much action yet! Luca did a quick register of everyone and again everyone was there raring to go. There was a tall lady dressed in full black abaya and niqab. Luca was very chatty with her. I assumed she was his local friend Fatimah. It must have been a good hour before Luca finally introduced me to her. She was very polite and seemed genuinely nice. That was a good start as it gave me faith that my visa would be sorted. There was a lot going on and thankfully Fatimah had brought her crew to help.

All I was assigned to do was cue the models when to walk and where to pose whilst the presenter talked about the outfits they were wearing. The models were great and had already had their hair and makeup done to save time. The girls walked with such elegance and attitude during the rehearsals. I felt proud to be working with them. The crew filming seemed much organised and on point. Everyone seemed to know what they were doing. I have to say, it was one of the most organised shoots I have been on. The presenter was from Lebanon and she had such charisma as she spoke. She enticed her audience. The fashion segment was up next so I did my last-minute checks. We were ready to roll. The first model went out and ended up holding her pose on the wrong position so we had to re-take the shot. Off they went on set, one by one, keeping composed and being professional. It was over so quickly.

They had other segments like sports and music but I didn't get too involved in that. I went to the kitchen that was provided for us and stuffed myself with the delicate coconut biscuits that were calling my name.

The day was beginning to drag as no-one in the other segments seemed to get it right in the first instance. It was fast approaching 8pm and they said the words that I had been waiting to hear for ages. It was a wrap. Before everyone disappeared, there was going to be a debriefing of the day and how it went and what would be the next step. There was a lot of constructive feed-back, the main issue being that some of the specialist presenters, i.e. the sports and health specialists needed to keep their links short sharp and sweet as they were waffling on too much and missing the point of what was needed to be said. Other than that, it was a success. Everyone performed very well. The show had cutting edge. It had to succeed!

On the way out, I briefly spoke to Fatimah who was very excited with the day's work. We agreed to meet in a week or so as she had a lot going on. I wanted to see her sooner than later because of my visa situation. In the taxi on the way back I told Luca that Fatimah said she would be busy for the next two weeks and that I needed to have my visa ASAP. No ifs or buts allowed. He said he would speak to her the following day as it had been a long day and she would not pick up her phone for sure. There was nothing else I wanted to say so I rested my eyes for a while and fell asleep.

My eyes opened exactly at the right minute as the car just pulled up near the apartment. I dragged myself out of the car then into the lift. It was always so quiet in the hallway. I never saw my neighbours or had any interaction with them. It was weird. I opened the door and the feeling of being home had never felt sweeter. I got changed into my pyjamas and headed straight to bed. I was too tired to even eat. The fact that Luca hadn't confirmed what day he was returning back to Lebanon was preying on my mind. The feeling of 'not knowing' was unsettling. As soon as my head hit the pillow I was knocked out.

I woke up about 2pm in the afternoon. I had really needed the rest. Luca was busy doing paper work at the table. I straight away reminded him that he must call Fatimah to speed things up. Time was of the essence. He said he would call her as soon as he finished his admin work. It was lunch time so I got ready and headed out for some food. There was a lovely Pakistani restaurant about a good fifteen minute-walk away. I had only been there once. It didn't look all that fancy from outside but the food was mouth-watering.

I knew exactly what I wanted to eat. I was in a serious mood for a very spicy lamb curry with fresh bread. For starters, I ordered pani puri which is what I call food shots.

There's a hollow shell that you fill with a spicy chick pea mix then you add the tamarind sauce and fill it to the top of the shell, then knock it back like a shot. It's like a party of different flavours in your mouth. The food tasted as good as it looked. I asked them to give me extra raw green chillies to eat with my food. I loved the heat. I had a very hard stomach and could handle practically anything! I was so stuffed but still managed to save a little room for dessert. I opted for ghajar halwa, which is a dish made with carrots, nuts, milk and cream. I remember when my mum used to make it. It took hours on end as it needed to be stirred for ages then cooked for a good length of time. It was delicious but I have to say my mum's version was unbeatable. Still, this was the next best thing and it was so fulfilling.

I rolled out of the restaurant and decided it would be nice to take a walk and burn off the massive number of calories I had just consumed. It was nice to take these walks and free my mind from thoughts. I loved to walk aimlessly and enjoy the sights on the way. Just as I was winding down, my phone rang. It was Luca. I didn't want to answer it. I wanted to enjoy these peaceful moments. Just as I put my phone back in my pocket it started to ring again. It was Luca again. I wondered what he wanted because he was always wanting and never giving. I couldn't be bothered so I switched my phone off. That was much better. I couldn't be harassed now.

A few hours later and feeling bit lighter from my very heavy lunch, I headed home. Luca was sat watching television. He said he tried to call me several times but I didn't pick up. He had spoken to Fatimah and she said that she would be able to sort my visa out sooner. She said she would send her cousin to pick up my passport from me and asked if we could meet him in the evening. Luca confirmed that we would be ok to meet. I told him that I didn't want random people coming to the apartment and that we should meet him outside somewhere. So, he messaged her to say that we would meet her cousin near the Dubai Museum at 7.30pm which would mean getting the boat across to the other side. I loved doing this journey every single time.

We were both watching television and I got a text message from my sister. I called her without even fully reading the text. I had been meaning to speak to her for a long time. I was lucky enough to speak to everyone as they were all at home. My mum asked how I was getting on with work. I said it was great and told her about the pilot show and my plans.

I didn't want to worry them with the fact that I still didn't have a visa and that the stamp on my passport was about to run out, or even that I was living with a selfish individual who had screwed me up financially and was actually living off me. They would worry unnecessarily even more so because of the distance. It would be all sorted soon anyway. I must have been on the phone for an hour. Every second was a quality moment.

I washed and got dressed and packed my passport in my bag. I had a photocopy of it which was filed away in my bag of documents which had my birth certificate and all my educational certificates. Luca was ready and so we headed out towards the boat area. It was quite light still and beautiful weather as always. There was a bit of small talk on the way, nothing too heavy. I was like a child when I sat on the boat. It felt like such a novelty. It made me smile.

We were just stepping off the boat when Luca's phone rang. The man we were meeting was running about ten minutes late. I just wanted this done and dusted. It had been prolonged for way too long. There was a really cute little shop a few yards up on the corner that sold real silver jewellery. I had been passed it a few times and not had time to have a look inside so this was a prime opportunity to do just that. We went inside and I asked to look at the men's rings. A treat day was over-due. The owner displayed some amazing pieces. There was one particular ring that stood out because of its simple elegant design. I tried it on and it fitted perfectly. All that was left to do was barter for a good price. I already had a price in my mind and it needed to match the price in the seller's mind. I went for it and didn't back down. He did and I got it for the price I wanted. That felt good! A job well done! I hadn't lost my touch!

We headed swiftly towards where the man was parked up. In front of me there was a stunning Ferrari with tinted windows, and beautiful sparkling silver alloys. Luca said that was the cousin's car. I didn't believe him until we went right up to the car. The window was wound down. The man inside the car seemed to recognise Luca and unlocked the door. It wasn't a normal door; it was the wing style door which went up instead of out. The interiors were equally stunning, black leather smooth and sexy. I said 'salaam', he replied and then I got into the car. My first every experience of being in a Ferrari! No longer a Ferrari virgin! The guy could only speak Arabic, so again, I was left to try and figure out what the conversation was about which wasn't much at all. He could only park there for a short time and so stopped the car in a more convenient place. I pulled out my passport. Luca took it and handed it over to the man.

Needless to say, I never saw my passport again.

Things seemed to be going from bad to worse. Still no visa and no sign of one either. I hounded Luca about three days after handing over my passport to some random person because by this time my visa had expired and to my extreme horror I had become an illegal immigrant! Never in my wildest dreams did I ever think that I would sink to this level.

I was a law-abiding citizen. This was so out of context. He didn't seem to care and just said that his friend Fatimah would take care of it. I kept on at him but still received nothing productive in return. A fat load of good he was! I was in deep, deep lumber. Luca's true colours were clearly evident. It was all about him. He had no care in the world for anyone other than himself! I was beginning to learn a lot of life's lessons in a short space of time.

One early evening I went out to get some groceries and Luca insisted on coming with me for some reason - there seemed to be hidden motives for everything! We had finished paying at the till and then Luca said we needed to get out of the shop as soon as possible because he had spotted a couple of policemen walking around the area. It was normal for them to do random check-ups and ask you to present your passport or even a photo copy of a passport. Unlike the UK, the photo copy of any document was nearly as precious as the original in the UAE. If I was to get stopped I could have potentially been imprisoned because I had no ID or even a photocopy on me. I did have a photocopy in my bag at home but then my visa was invalid and so I could have been issued with a one-way ticket to jail which was a traumatic thought! Even though I am a British citizen and I sound like one, I do not look like a conventional British person. It felt so degrading having to dodge the policemen.

Why was I being punished? I hadn't even done anything wrong apart from trust a stranger! We managed to get home without being caught and the realisation of this trauma was taking its toll. I let loose on Luca. It was his fault, he had led me to believe he was competent and honest enough to sort my visa but I could not have been more wrong. He tried to calm me down by saying it would be sorted and that he had given me his word. Well, that was not good enough to me anymore. Anyone can talk the talk. I needed to see physical results and not this crap coming out of his dishonest mouth!

He then came up with the most bizarre idea. He said that my friend Shahin's visa would still be in date. I looked at him thinking what on God's earth has that got to do with anything.

He carried on saying that I should ask her to email me her visa stamp and that he would manipulate it onto my passport photocopy. I was in full rage now! My voice rose to great heights as my patience was non-existent. How dare he stoop to that level? It was because of him I was in that situation. I could not believe the way his mind was functioning. Only a crafty, dishonest thief could think of something as extreme as that! I didn't care how desperate I was and by this stage I was very desperate.

I was not going to take part in some dodgy act! He tried his best to convince me but I insisted that would never happen in a million years and that he should just get it sorted the proper way, as he had promised me originally.

He still hadn't given me a date as to when he was leaving. I wanted him out for good! He had totally outstayed his welcome a long time ago. In a way, I felt trapped and suffocated. I didn't have anyone I could go to or anyone that I could speak to openly about this surreal situation. I then tried my luck again and asked him when he was going to be leaving. He looked me in the eye and said 'soon' then just gave me an evil smirk. Still none the wiser, I had to keep positive as surely this could not carry on forever. The truth of the matter was that I was now confined to the four walls for certain times of the day. The thought of not having the independence of staying out till whatever time I wanted was extremely daunting and horrifying. That was the harsh reality. The only thing I was not restricted from was sleeping.

CHAPTER 13

It was quite early in the morning and I could hear lots of rustling of bags. I looked up and to my ultimate disbelief I saw Luca with his bags all packed. He was dressed very smartly in what looked like a brand new expensive outfit. His bags were all neatly put in position ready to be picked up. He said that he was returning to Lebanon and that someone would be in touch regarding my visa. He picked up his bags and went. My jaw was still on the floor from shock. When the door shut behind him it felt like all the negativity was leaving with him too. I opened the door to make sure that he had gone. The coast was clear. I shut the door and took a huge sigh of relief then went back to bed. It was truly a very blissful moment. Finally, it was time to say good riddance to bad rubbish!

I slept for a good few healthy hours. My eyes opened around 3pm. I lay in bed for a further few minutes watching television but appreciating the calmness of the atmosphere. It was all my space, my apartment! Never to be shared. Feeling very content from inside, I got up, showered and got dressed. I then put the kettle on to have a cuppa. The tea tasted great as I had started to buy the evaporated milk and used it in my tea and coffee. I sat down comfortably on the sofa. I was so relaxed.

Suddenly the door-bell rang. I jumped. I wasn't expecting anyone so I was very curious to know who it was. As I opened the door, I was pushed back at great speed. I went flying back and landed on the table which then gave way, causing me to fall backwards hurting my back. I didn't know what was going on. For a few seconds, I wasn't able to recollect where I was. It was like having an out of body experience. I was there but not there. I froze with fright. A very surreal experience! I just about managed to get myself up from the table but then the man that pushed me violently grabbed me by my collar and started shouting, 'Where is Luca?'

He had company as there were three other men. The one that pushed me was very tall and very broad and stocky. He must have been about 6.4" thereabouts. One of his accomplices was similar height and the other two were shorter but very stocky built. I tried so hard to recollect where I had seen them. Suddenly it clicked.

They had all been at the pilot shoot. I had previously seen them but never really talked to them. It was Luca that had dealt with them. I had found them very unapproachable and hugely intimidating!

The ring leader kept shouting and his tone was getting louder and more aggressive. He punched my left cheek so hard that I couldn't feel my face. It left a tingling sensation. I really thought that my teeth were broken. He didn't even give me an opportunity to speak. I tried to tell them that he had gone back to Beirut. I just wanted to know why they were behaving the way they were. I didn't have anything to do with them. It wasn't making any sense. I could not believe what was happening! Then he said that he wanted his money back there and then. The situation was getting more confusing by the second. I asked, 'what money?' and he said it was the money that was stolen from him. I said I didn't know about any money and said that Luca just lived here. I didn't know of his whereabouts or what he had been up to. The other men looked like they were ready to kill. I felt the anger in their eyes. They meant business and they weren't going anywhere until this was sorted!

I was so scared. I was beginning to fear the worst. If they killed me no one would even know of my existence. I didn't know anybody else there. My passport had gone. I would only ever be discovered if the landlord hadn't heard from me for a while and that would only be because he would be chasing up his rent. The reality of the whole situation was sinking in. I pleaded with them. I had no idea about the money but they were insisting that I had it. I didn't understand what this money was for. I kept saying I had no idea. He then screamed, swearing violently that Luca had promised them to sort their visas out. He had taken cash money up to the value of £2000 per person, bearing in mind there were about fifty people. That was a lot of money he had accumulated in a very short space of time.

I tried to explain that he had done the exact same with me. They would not have it. I couldn't even get a word in edge ways. There it came again, another unexpected punch to my face! I was in severe pain. It was not worth the risk trying to challenge these people. I had no chance against them but I still wasn't giving up and tried to reason with them. I remember so vividly how he grabbed my throat and started to squeeze it tight. He screamed at me, threatening that if I didn't get the money they would kill me and cut me up into pieces and that nobody would know of my existence! I was panicking like crazy, moving up and down like fish out of water. I couldn't breathe. To be told that I could potentially be murdered was the most horrifying thing my ears had ever heard! This was it. My life was ending!

He reluctantly let go of me and said something in Arabic to the other three men. I was still struggling to breathe at this point and trying to make head or tail of what was happening. I couldn't focus.

Following instructions from the ring leader, they started to trash my apartment. They headed towards the wardrobe and pulled everything out. Strangely enough, even the few things I had in the fridge like milk, cheese and bread all came flying out onto the floor. One of the shorter men spotted my bag that contained all my documents. He snatched it and stuffed it with my brother's digital camera, walkman, my designer belts and everything else they thought was of value. My eyes were drowned with tears.

It was like my life was flashing before my very eyes. They managed to find my wallet. I must have had about £1000 worth of cash in Dirhams which went straight into the pocket of the ring leader. I was spitting venom at the fact that Luca literally committed an act of fraud and left me to pick up the pieces. He had taken people's hard-earned money and blatantly lied to them by promising them something he had no intention of delivering. What an evil person! This was not fair on me at all. This was my reward for being an honest and trusting person. I started to blame myself. I should have been more vigilant. The signs were there but I had been too gullible and innocent to even notice.

They seriously were not going anywhere! By accident I took a glimpse of myself in the mirror and I was petrified at the sight of myself. My face was covered in blood. I was doomed in Dubai! It was heart-breaking seeing the state of the apartment. They showed no remorse whatsoever. They all kept screaming and shouting, predominantly in Arabic. I didn't know what to think or what their next move would be. It was the most terrifying moment of my life! I have always hated confrontation and always stayed away from it. I was in the midst of something horrifically serious. There wasn't a way out! The main man had held me by the back of my neck all this time. He pushed me onto the sofa like I was some kind of rag. I was shaking like a leaf. I didn't dare look them in the eye. The shouting was so over whelming and unbearable. It went on for forever.

Eventually the noise level dropped. I was very surprised that the neighbours didn't come knocking to see what all the noise was about. To be honest I never even knew who the neighbours were. There was never anyone around.

I had the main guy literally in my face at this point whilst the others gathered around close. He said that they would get the money out of me no matter what they had to do!

One of the shorter guys propped up the table whilst the other shorter man found a pen and a piece of paper.

The main man slammed the paper and pen on the table and said that I had to write down word for word of what was going to be said. I had no idea where this was going. My mind was all over the place. The stress and anxiety was hugely intense. It just seemed best to go with what they said because nothing was adding up and that I didn't have a choice in the matter anyway.

The main man started to shout rather than speak. He said that I needed to write that I owed the four men the equivalent of £8000 and that I would have to pay them as soon as possible. They also wanted my father's name in full and my address in the UK. I was forced to sign and date it. He said that this bound as a legal contract and that if I didn't get this payment sorted by the next day then I would be thrown into the cells of Dubai. He said once I was in jail I would never be released and that I would rot in there till I died! He also said that the police would never believe my version of the story. The thought of this gave me uncontrollable shivers. How did they expect me to get such a large amount of money in such a short space of time? In my head, I had exhausted every option of how to get the funds. I had to face the fact that I couldn't do this which meant my days were numbered in this world!

The thought that I would never see my family again was hurting my soul. I had failed! I was a failure! I had let everyone down! I was no good to the world anyway! These thoughts kept circulating in my head. They wouldn't even let me go to the bathroom. I just had to sit there and be told what to do and when to do it. The other tall man didn't seem as vocal as the others. I don't know why but I felt deep down he believed my story. If that was the case then he should have talked the others out of putting me through this hell that I was experiencing. In reality, they were all as guilty as each other. The main man was still no calmer and said that if I didn't sort this mess out, he would teach me a lesson. I dreaded to think what that would be!

They had been here for several hours now. I was officially held hostage in my own apartment. My phone rang and the leader checked to see who was calling me just in case it was Luca. It was my mum calling from the UK. My heart sank. He cut the call and switched it off and put it in the bag with the rest of the stuff. I hadn't eaten all day and was feeling very weak, but that was the least of my problems. The main man dragged me up like I was an animal and pulled my head right back. I let out a scream as it really hurt.

Again, he wrapped his hands around my neck and said that they would leave now and that they will be returning the next day. He reminded me of what would happen if I didn't get the money. His piercing tone of voice sent shivers down my spine. I knew that I had to act on their words. I froze on the spot. I was in a foreign country as an illegal immigrant. I didn't know of anyone that would be able to help me. I had to get hold of some money somehow, but how? They had taken practically everything. I was left with nothing. The main man screamed in my face once last time before he started to get violent again.

He kicked me in the stomach and I immediately ended up on the floor in a crouch position and then he went for another kick. He was acting like a seriously deranged animal. The other tall man had to drag him away. I was seriously damaged. The door slammed behind them. I was crying like a helpless child, laid on the floor. The pain was excruciating. I didn't know what to do. I didn't have a phone or any money. I had lost everything. I had really hit rock bottom. There was no way out! My mind was over cluttered with thoughts and fear. I could not think properly. For the rest of the night I just lay on the floor whimpering.

Morning came after what seemed like a very long time. The aches and pain where even more evident. I felt completely helpless. I had urinated in my pants. I had shattered into a billion pieces. My life had turned from being perfect to a nightmare beyond repair. Very slowly I managed to get myself up off the floor. Every movement was a huge effort. The apartment looked like a bomb site. It was the least of my problems. One step at a time was all I could handle both physically and mentally. I needed to wash myself. I was grateful for the body wash and shampoo in the bathroom. A couple of outfits in the washing basket, some toiletries, a cap, one pair of trainers and not forgetting my portfolios were all I had to my name. Everything else had been swiped away from my very eyes. I had no money no phone, nothing!

It took more than three times as long to wash myself. I tried to tidy my face up as much as I could. I grabbed a t-shirt and a pair of jeans from the dirty laundry basket and managed to put them on with great difficulty. Then I slowly headed towards the sofa and sank in trying to get as comfortable as possible which wasn't very. My mind was a complete blank. I couldn't think. I was feeling too frail and scared to go out! The shock factor was too high. I needed some time to not think but to rest.

I fell asleep for a good few hours. When I got up I didn't feel any pain for the first few seconds and then it kicked in.

There was no way I could get the money. I didn't have any resources to do anything. Thinking of all this put me into panic mode. I started talking to myself trying to figure out how to sort this. Every thought just took me towards a brick wall. It hurt to think. I was finished!

All I wanted to do is sleep again and wake up with this nightmare not existing. Just as my eyes shut again the door-bell rang. My heart beat so fast. I was getting palpitations. My body froze. I was angry with myself because I should have gone to the police station but then I would have been in trouble with them due to having no passport and being an illegal immigrant.

If I had explained it all to the police, maybe they would have understood and helped me? Who knows? I was trapped either way. Besides it was way too late now anyway. I had missed my opportunity.

The bell was ringing consistently and the knocking on the door was getting louder and more aggressive. I walked towards the front door with my heart in my stomach. I was shaking uncontrollably. It felt like every step I took towards the door was closer to my death! It took a lot of attempts to open the door because my hands were shaking so much. As soon as I opened the door, in they came as violently as the day before.

The main man grabbed my neck and gave it a good hard squeeze. I wasn't able to breathe. Then he let go and I got my breath back. It was the same four people. The most perverted thing was that the main guy came in wearing my designer belt and he had my walk-man in his pocket. Their facial expressions were much more frightening today. I was so scared. I hadn't realised what the time was as I had slept more than I had thought. It was late afternoon and they wanted their money. I tried to explain that I didn't have a phone or any way of contacting anyone and that I needed more time. Maybe by some miracle I could get the money together? It was worth trying to buy more time but they just were not being fair in any way. Every time I tried to say something he would talk over me. There was no allowance for any explanation.

We were all stood up but I was on the floor in no time as one of the shorter men burst into a rage and started attacking me. He was violently kicking me and punching me. I tried to defend myself by putting my hands in front of my face. The others were cheering him on. This was it for me. The pain was too much to bear. The main man said he meant what he said and that he was going to teach me lesson I would never forget. He was so big, and there was me like a rake in comparison. He dragged me by the collar and threw me onto the bed. The others followed and headed towards the bed. I didn't know what was happening. The two shorter guys clamped my arms down with their weight which restricted my movement.

It suddenly dawned on me what may be happening. I moved every sore bit of me trying to release myself. I started to scream as loud as I could. The other tall man was on standby. I lay there fearing for my life. The main man was standing in front of me. He managed to keep my legs locked down but even then, I moved. I couldn't believe what was about to happen to me. The main man began to unzip his trousers. My cries and screams were getting louder and more hysterical. He was getting closer. He loosened his grip on my leg and I took full advantage of that and kicked him hard in the face. That was it. He turned into a wild animal. He instructed the man on standby to pin my right leg down as he gripped my left leg. I kept resisting and fighting.

It got to the point where the shorter man on my left stuck his hand over my mouth to drown my screaming. I kept fighting but slowly became weaker and unable to breathe properly. I had lost! The main man viciously thrust himself in me deep! My body flung in the air like a dead corpse releasing a final spasm. The more I resisted the more pain I endured. He carried on, enjoying every ounce of pain he was inflicting on me. I eventually stopped resisting and lay there dead. I didn't feel anything anymore. They couldn't do any more harm to me because I had taken the worst of it. In fact, I was hoping that was it for me. I was happy and ready to embrace death. At least I would be relieved of such pain! I had cried all I could cry as my tears had dried up. I felt hollow. I didn't feel anything anymore. Finally, they released me. My arms and legs just flopped on the bed. My eyes were just fixated to the ceiling. Then main man came close to me and screamed something at me but I couldn't understand him. It was all blurred. I was seeing black and that was it!

I must have passed out for some time. For a moment, I didn't know where I was. I very slowly came around. I remember looking around the room and seeing all the mess. I couldn't move. My whole body was paining. I went into a foetus position and started to cry for my mum. I couldn't stop. I didn't have the strength to do anything. I hadn't eaten for about two days. My body had been severely battered. I carried on staring at the ceiling for comfort. I needed my family around me but I didn't think myself of being worthy of being around them. I was dirty. I mean really, I could have resisted more? My body had frozen but still I could have done more. I could have tried harder!

This was all beginning to run through my head. I was so upset and angry with myself. I hated myself so much at this point!

It was one thing being beaten up but how could the other thing have happened. I was a man, it didn't happen to men. I couldn't say the word.

It was one of those horrific moments where I knew I had to get up and pull myself together but I couldn't because it happened to me. I had been raped. As the obscene word came to mind I started to cry more and harder.

It was not safe for me to stay here. If I did, I knew I would not live to see the next day. I needed to be strong somehow but I just couldn't. I lay back down lifeless. I was going nowhere for now. Time was moving fast and as difficult as it was for me, I had to do something and do it quick. I was struggling to think clearly. First things first! I very slowly manoeuvred myself off the bed. As I moved, there seemed to be a trail of blood that I was leaving behind. I felt sick, disgusted and dirty all over again.

I had never experienced such horrific pain like this in my life. I could say with complete confidence that I was a broken man physically and mentally.

As I headed towards the bathroom at the pace of a slug, jeans down my ankles, I was racking my brains trying to think of who I could contact. It was so difficult. Then I remembered there was one person that I could contact, Maher who was Luca's friend. He had seemed nice but what if he was like Luca? What if he too was a fraudster and a dishonest person who enjoyed using people? Let's be honest I literally had nothing to lose. The strangest thing was that I always remembered Maher's number. It was one of those easy numbers that always stuck in my mind. The question was how I could possibly get in contact with him?

Before thinking any further, I needed to make myself look more presentable. I washed myself and had to wear the same clothes because I didn't have anything else. I didn't care as long I was wearing something. I was lucky that those evil people that should not be allowed to be called humans had left my model bag which was in the bathroom. It had a concealer stick in there given to me by a lovely makeup artist that I had met on a shoot. I covered up the worst bits of my face; my left cheek and forehead. I didn't look too scary now, thankfully. I put on my cap and was ready to start thinking of a plan. I could not afford to waste even a second. I had officially hit rock bottom and the only way was up! I had no money at all. I don't know what came over me but I started to look around the apartment for a Dirham. There's always that one coin knocking around somewhere. I searched the whole place but there was nothing to be found.

Just as I was beginning to lose hope, I found a telephone calling card right at the back of the sideboard. In Dubai, you have to purchase cards to use in normal public phone booths. I had nothing to lose so I headed to a phone booth not too far away from me.

I started dialling the numbers and thank God there was some credit on it. This was truly a huge miracle. My heart beat was racing crazily and then I finally heard Maher's voice.

I got very emotional but had to pull myself together because the credit could have finished any second. I briefly told him what Luca had done and that I was getting death threats from these vicious people. To my ultimate surprise he said that I should take whatever belongings I had and make my way towards his flat. I must admit I was very nervous as I had only seen him a couple of times. He seemed nice but then didn't they all! I didn't know what kind of person he really was but I didn't have anything to lose or any choice. I had a very strong feeling that the gang would be back again. I said that I would go home, get my things and head to his place. The great thing was that his flat was walking distance from mine.

I suddenly felt some inner strength. I didn't have time to feel sorry for myself. I had to be quick and be extremely productive with my very little time.

I got home, threw my things in a carrier bag, then locked up and left. I knocked on my neighbour's doors both on my right and left just to tell them to call the police if any men were seen knocking on my door but as usual no one answered. Thankfully, as I was heading to the lift I saw the caretaker for the building. I explained to him that should he see any men hovering around my door that he must call the police. They were dangerous!

I was feeling so on edge because I kept thinking that any minute I would bump into them and that would truly be the end of me. It's impossible to describe the exact feeling. I was feeling nervous, anxious, scared and relieved all in one go. I got out of the building with ease and started walking in the direction of Maher's flat. He gave very precise directions which gave me a good indication as to where he was based. Even though I was in agony, I walked as fast as I could. I had to! Every minute seemed to take an hour. I would keep looking back anxiously just to make sure I wasn't being followed. I would jump at the sight of anyone behind me. I couldn't believe that I had made it into Maher's road. I stopped to take a deep breath. I was finally in a safe zone. I could see Maher from a short distance. He came running towards me. He was so shocked seeing me in the state I was in. When I first met him, I was full of life. I looked like a model and I was a very confident and sorted guy. He could not believe the extreme change in me.

It was almost as if he was going to cry because he felt such pity at the state I was in. He kindly took my bag and invited me to his very cosy flat. He said I looked as if I was starved. He wasn't wrong.

He let me settle in as he went down to the shop that was on his doorstep and got me a chicken sandwich. I savoured every bite! I told him exactly what had happened. He could not believe how Luca had done the dirty on me. I also learned that Maher is Luca's neighbour in Lebanon and that's how they came to know each other. The most shocking thing was that apparently Luca was a known scammer back home. The most scandalous thing he did, other than screw me and many others over was that he stole from a charity. He conned them and scammed them. He had mastered it to a fine art. What a shameless disgusting individual. Karma was sure on the cards for him. I prayed from the heart that he would get his comeuppance sooner rather than later. I despised this so called human being.

I couldn't bring myself to tell Maher of the sexual assault that I had suffered. I didn't know how he would react. I didn't want to push it. I wanted to build my strength and get myself sorted. That was the biggest priority. Maher said to get a good night's sleep. He was very comforting and said that he would help me get out of this situation and we would work on a plan. I made it clear to him that I wanted to go back home. The thought of home brought tears to my eyes. It was official to say that I had had enough of Dubai and I wanted to be home with my family!

CHAPTER 14

For a few days, I stayed put in Maher's flat. I didn't want to face the world outside. His friends came in and out and were so kind. They would offer to take me out to restaurants and pay for me. This was restoring a bit of faith that humanity did exist. I was happy just snuggling up in a duvet watching films on television. He even let me borrow his clothes which I really appreciated. I was still quite scared of going out on my own. I kept thinking that the evil gang would find me and finish me off for good. I didn't want to take any unnecessary risks.

Maher worked in a clothing shop located in a mall quite close by. He would go to work and I would stay at home. That would be the routine. Then randomly one day there was a fashion segment on television where they were showing catwalk shows from around the world and I realised that I had left my portfolios in my apartment. I tried not to blame myself as I did leave in a hurry. I wanted them. I know it didn't seem hugely important in the bigger scheme of things but I had worked damn hard. My life was in those two books. I had to get them.

That evening when Maher came I told him that I needed to go back to my apartment. He said I should only go if I really needed to. I felt I did. The bruises on my face and body were very slowly clearing up. I had very sensitive skin and whenever I hurt myself, it would always take ages to heal. It was no way near as bad as the first day I arrived at Maher's. My stubbornness was kicking in and so I decided that I would go to get my portfolios quite early in the morning. Surely, they wouldn't be there so early, would they?

I left Maher's flat at about 7.30am. It felt so strange being out. For so many days I had only seen daylight through a tiny window. I was constantly having battles with myself. I was feeling brave one minute and then my weak side would kick in. Only God knows how I was feeling when I headed out that day! I had been clear of any negative signs so far. I got into the lift of my building and the vigorous shaking started. I briskly walked to my apartment, opened the door and then locked it behind me as quickly as I could. My portfolios had fallen to the side of the sideboard. I picked them up and walked towards the front door. My heart was racing. I put my ear against the door to see if I could hear anything. It was silent. I let myself out, locked the door and headed for the lift which seemed to take forever to come. The lift stopped on my floor and I froze in fright. The doors of the lift opened and my heart stopped.

It was the caretaker who walked out of the lift. I was covered in sweat. My heart started beating again. I was ecstatic that it was him that came out of the lift and no one else. I asked him if anyone had been hanging around my door and he said yes! There were four men that had been coming on a daily basis. They had asked him about me. He denied having any knowledge. They would wait for a good forty minutes or so then leave. I stressed to the caretaker that he must call the police should he see them again. I finished my conversation immediately and headed out back to Maher's. I could not believe that they had been round again and again! I was petrified. I moved as quickly as I could and got to Maher's flat safe and sound!

I had made myself quite at home at Maher's; he was definitely the host with the most. He asked me if I felt strong enough to speak to my family. They needed to know what had happened but not the finer details. I needed money too as I couldn't continue to live off Maher who not once complained about anything, bless him. Later that day, I decided to take the plunge and call my family. Maher very kindly let me use his mobile phone to make the call. I dialled very nervously. I had no idea what I was going to say but I had to say something. It was ringing. At any moment, someone was going to pick up! It was my mum. She kept saying 'hello' but I had lost my voice. I tried so hard to speak but nothing would come out of my mouth. I was numb! She kept saying 'hello' and as I listened to her voice the tears came rolling down. She knew it was me and kept asking me if I was ok. I could hear more voices in the background and naturally everyone seemed disturbed by the phone call.

Finally, through the tears, I managed to string a few words together. When asked again if I was ok I couldn't lie and I said that I wasn't. I briefly talked through the situation. That set my mum off and she was crying which made me more emotional. I spoke to my sister and my aunt Afshan who also seemed disturbed but they had more control of their emotions. At this stage I was a bit more together and able to explain myself better.

I was so happy that I had plucked up the courage to call my family because I got all the assurances that I needed. It made me bond with members of my family even more strongly than before. The call ended on a more positive note which gave me hope that things would be getting better. I felt a load being lifted from my chest. My aunt said not to worry and that she would arrange to send some money over so I could get a phone and sort my costs for replacing my passport which was another headache that I had to contend with. The funds would be enough to cover me for the rest of my stay which I was wishing would be shorter rather than longer. If I needed more, that would be arranged. At this point it was impossible to even take a wild guess as to how long I would be staying in Dubai.

Having talked in depth to Maher the plan was once I got the money through from my aunt, I needed to head to the British Embassy. Apparently, they would be able to issue me with a passport so I could head back to the UK. In theory, it seemed quite straight forward. I was praying that it would be just as simple in practice. It was best to take each day at a time.

It was nice that I could keep in contact with my family on a regular basis as they would call me on Maher's phone. I needed that contact so badly to keep me sane.

The best way for the money to get to me was for it to be sent via Western Union. I didn't have any form of ID so I was relying on Maher, which in all honesty made me a bit nervous. What if he took the money for himself? The thought did cross my mind but he had been so good to me. Surely, he wouldn't pull a stunt like that? Again, it was a risk I simply had to take!

Early next morning, I text messaged my aunt to send the money and told her that Maher would use his ID to get it. It was very early hours in the UK. By the time she read the message it would be much later in Dubai. Maher headed to work whilst I stayed in bed resting up as much as I could. I was to meet Maher at his workplace at lunchtime so that we could go to get the money. He always had a late lunch which was perfect time-wise for me. I washed and dressed and made my way out to the mall. I had noticed that my body was changing, my face was very gaunt, and my frame was thinning by the day. I had hugely lost my appetite and was eating minimally just for the sake of it. It was quite a refreshing walk. I would only go out if it was compulsory. I was forever grateful that my family were all pitching in to support me financially in my time of need. I hated being dependant. I had always been independent. The funds would help enormously. I had borrowed some money from Maher and so returning that would be the first thing I did.

I got to the shop where Maher was busy at work, working his charms on a very beautiful Arab lady that was indecisive about what style of jeans to buy. Within no time the jeans were in a bag and in her hands. He was highly skilled in his job. The lady left the shop and he put the closed sign up in the window and then we headed out to the money exchange shop. Maher was always on such a good level which helped me to stay positive. Just a few yards away and we had arrived at our destination. It was a tiny little shop full of people shouting and being extremely noisy. This was making me feel very uncomfortable. The nerves were kicking in too. We had to push our way past the people. The man on the counter was quite stern looking.

It made me even more nervous. Maher had received the relevant details to get the authorization. The transaction was straightforward thankfully. The man counted the money and it was exactly what I was expecting. Maher straight away handed the money over to me which was a huge relief. I handed over to him the amount that he had lent me and then we headed out for some lunch which was on me.

We had to shovel down the food as Maher needed to get back to work and I needed to buy a mobile phone. I went into the nearest shop and got a small phone. It looked really cool because it had all the Arabic alphabet and numbers. The Arabic lettering is so beautiful and elegant. The feeling of being able to go in a shop and buy something with my own money was an amazing and satisfying feeling. I guess technically it wasn't my own money but it was a start. I would never expect that from my family normally but I was in desperate need. I could picture the face of some of my family members having to contribute. They would have hated to part with their pennies. I think some of them would have been happy for me to suffer rather than give a small amount of their money away if they had the choice!

I felt that I had achieved a lot on that day. However, there were clearly more obstacles to face. The journey hadn't even started.

CHAPTER 15

Another day, another challenge! I had packed up my belongings in a small travel bag that I had bargained hard for at a little market stall near the flat. I had my brand-new phone which I was really proud of. I had blasted out text messages to everyone who needed to have my number. At least I was contactable at any time now. Today was going to be a big day for me as I was going to the British Embassy. I had heard that they are very efficient and that I would be on my way home in no time. My hopes were raised extremely high. It was good to remain positive.

The Embassy was a bit of a walk but I didn't mind it at all. My confidence to walk around by myself was on the up. However, I still found myself looking behind from time to time. I had to literally watch my back.

After getting a bit lost I managed to find the Embassy, a big official looking building. I walked in very nervously. I briefly explained that I no longer had my passport and that I needed to see someone urgently. I was asked to take a seat. My eyes were wondering around the room. I felt very uncomfortable. I went into a bit of a daze and suddenly felt a gentle tap on my shoulder. I jumped out of my skin but then felt calmer as I was greeted with a very friendly smile by a lady who was one of the case officers. She could tell how distressed I was and reassured me that she was there to help me. It was upsetting and frustrating having to go through the whole story again and again. She listened with great sincerity. I said that I wanted my new passport as soon as possible so that I could leave late that evening or early hours of the morning. Then she burst my bubble saying that there was no way I would be leaving that early and that there would be a full investigation carried out as my passport would be considered stolen. My heart was in my stomach. My eyes filled up with tears as I tried to hold them back. Why had I been told by people that this would be simple and that I would be on my way soon? I felt like I had died all over again! But she was doing her job and it was not in any way her fault. At least I now had a more realistic overview even though it hurt my soul! Her name was Caroline, a middle aged British lady. I had only just met her but I believed in her. She assured me with confidence that things would eventually be sorted. I wanted results there and then! That was clearly not going to happen. Caroline asked me if I wanted to speak to my family. I said yes and she dialled the number for me and let me call home using their phone.

I explained to my mum that it wasn't going to be as straight forward as I had initially hoped but I was in good hands and that it was simply a waiting game.

Caroline said they would not be able to issue me with a passport. I would need to report it missing at the police station and they would issue me with a statement of confirmation which would then enable the Embassy to issue me with another passport. It was all long winded. I had to prepare myself somehow for another rough ride. I had no idea how the system worked here but I was sure going to learn. Caroline gave me her card with all her details on it and she stressed that I could call her anytime I needed which was consoling. I left the Embassy totally heartbroken. I needed to wipe out any thought from my mind that suggested this was going to be straight forward. It sure wasn't going to be!

I headed towards the police station closest to my location. It was a big beige coloured building with steps leading to the main entrance. I felt like such a low life having to go into a police station even though I hadn't done anything. I walked in and it was not the prettiest of sites. I guess police stations are not supposed to look like five star hotels! I walked up to the reception counter like a lost puppy. I summarised that I had my passport stolen and that it needed to be reported. I had visited the Embassy and they had advised me to come to the police station to register the crime.

I was told to sit on the bench and wait for an officer to come. I was so scared. There were lots of corridors leading to lots of rooms. I dreaded to think what the cells were like. I was amused by the Arabs speaking in Hindi. Opposite me were a line of people who had blatantly committed a crime. They seemed quite disturbed and were making a lot of noise. An officer scolded them and told them to shut up. It was traumatising for me to witness.

Three hours later and I was still in the exact same position. No one had come to see me or given me any updates of what was happening. I went back to reception to ask and was told that they were very busy and that I would be attended to soon. I didn't dare dispute that. I wasn't going to chance my luck, so back I went into my seat obediently.

Five hours later, just as I was dropping off in my very uncomfortable seat, an officer came and asked me to follow him into one of the rooms. The room was not very big but had high ceilings with a big fan dangling down from it. The colours of the room were very subdued and lacked character. I sat down and started with my story.

He listened whilst doing some of his admin work. He then asked me if I had a number for Luca. I gave him the number I had. He called that number right in front of me. He managed to get through. He was speaking in Arabic and per usual I had no idea what they were talking was about. His tone was very stern. A few minutes later he hung up and told me that there was no person by the name of Luca Hadad. I was in complete shock. He said that the phone belonged to an elderly man and the person that picked up was his grandson Abdullah. I explained to the officer that was the number Luca was using in Dubai.

He then moved onto me and where I was from, asking if I really was from the UK. I know I don't look conventionally British but I have a strong northern accent. How could he have any doubt? We seemed to be stuck in a loop as he was asking me the same questions but using different words each time for variety! I was looking and feeling faint and so he asked me if I wanted to eat something. I said yes. He ordered a burger for me and said that we would break for about thirty minutes then continue.

I ate my burger quickly and sat back in the waiting area. Thirty minutes had long passed and there was no sign of the officer. I ended up waiting another frustrating three hours only for him to say that I should come back at 7am in the morning. I was so angry. What a waste of day and with nothing to show for it. I had no choice. I had to come back for more tomorrow. It was late. I felt that I hadn't had much daylight that day. That one day at the station had been hugely testing. I hoped that the following day would be short and sweet and more productive. On that note, I headed back to the flat. Maher was home from work and I updated him with the latest. There wasn't much to report to be honest. Maher said just to hang in there and roll with it. It was best not to stress myself out anymore. I needed to be strong and get on with it. It was definitely easier said than done!

So off I went in the morning at 6.30am in order to get there before 7am. I was working on UK time in terms of punctuality. It seemed to have skipped my mind that I was working against Dubai time. I got there ten minutes before. I spoke to the gentleman at reception. He remembered me from the previous day. He asked me to sit down and wait for an officer to come. Five hours later a different officer came over to me and led me to the same room. He started with the questioning and I had to run through the whole story again. He took notes. He was asking about my family history and where in the UK I lived. He was a bit too relaxed about the whole situation. It was like we had all the time in the world. They might have had, I most certainly didn't. I wanted to get back home. I wasn't going to go anywhere if we would be progressing at this sluggish pace.

There was another break. I was offered drinks and some hot food again. I wasn't feeling too hungry but forced myself to eat because I needed the strength to get through this traumatic day. I then sat back down in the waiting area. I waited another four hours then was called into the same room with the same officer. He wanted to know my address and said that we would be paying a visit to my apartment at some point. I am pretty sure I had given my full address previously. No problem, I was happy to comply even though the frustrations were beginning to kick in. After a brief conversation, it was time to sit back in my seat in the waiting area. Another hour had passed and eventually come 6pm, I was able to leave. I had been there for eleven hours.

This carried on for two whole weeks. I was losing the will to live as there wasn't any progression at all. I would have to go in, spend a ridiculous amount of time telling the same story to different people, waiting for endless hours in the waiting area then go home. I felt like I was working a double shift there. It was horrific. I could see no end. After another long shift at the station I thought I would call my mum from the phone booth just outside the station. I was feeling and looking extremely weak. My weight was falling off me. I was losing hair due to the stress. I was a complete mess. I had never in my life reached such a low point. I dialled the number and my mum picked up the phone. She asked me how I was, and I was silent for a few long seconds. She kept asking if I was there. I broke down and burst into tears. I so vividly remember saying to her that I am not coming back and that she will never see me again. It had all taken its toll on me. I couldn't handle the situation anymore. I wasn't moving forward, I was stationed in that one terrifying position. Naturally she was very emotional and trying her best to keep my spirits high. I had to end the conversation sooner than I would have liked to. It was all too much. I carried on crying in the phone booth for a few more minutes then headed back to the flat feeling upset and so pessimistic about my future. I got in and threw myself onto the bed with my head buried in the pillow as the tears started all over again.

About three hours later Maher came back from work with some food. I wasn't feeling hungry in the least but he had made such a huge effort, I didn't want to appear ungrateful. We ate our falafels and salad. He asked me how my day had been. It was obvious from my tone of voice that it had not been a good one. He then diverted the conversation towards the food and the interesting characters that had come into his shop.

Another morning, another day at the cop shop! No expectations whatsoever! The same old boring routine! The weird thing was that it was beginning to feel the norm. I went to reception and sat in my usual seat. I am sure if you would have looked closer you would have been able to see my bum print on the seat. It was firmly mine without a shadow of a doubt. I waited for about an hour and finally got seen by the same officer as I did the previous day. The fact that we had started early and I saw one person twice was a break through! We seated ourselves in the same little room. Today the air seemed different and I was feeling a little bit more positive. The officer wanted a full-blown description of Luca. I described him right down to every tiny detail. He then pulled out several photographs of men from his drawer. He placed them on the table and asked me if any of the photographs were of Luca. It didn't take me long because unfortunately to my disappointment none of them were Luca. He then said that he wanted to take a look at my apartment so he went to sort the vehicle out whilst I waited in the reception area. He came to collect me from reception and I sat in the back seat of a 4x4 vehicle with full black leather interiors and tinted windows.

I had never ever sat in a police vehicle. This was definitely a first. I felt uncomfortable throughout the journey. The officer had a colleague sat in the passenger seat beside him which made me more nervous for some strange reason. We got out of the car and I led the way to my apartment. They came in and looked shocked at the state of the place. It was upside down. They gave it a thorough look all over. I had no idea what they were looking for. It didn't take long and we were out of there. I had a gut feeling that was the last time I was going to see my apartment. I felt both sad and happy at the same time.

When I got into the car, the officer wanted the number of my landlord. He didn't specify why. I didn't want Faizel to be involved; it wasn't his fault, as he had nothing to do with this mess! The next stop was to be the flat where I was currently staying. Again, the mind boggled as to why they wanted to have a nosey at where I was staying. Maher was at work which I was so glad about. They came to the top of the stairs where the flat was. They asked if Maher was home. I said he was at work and that was it. I was free for the rest of the day. I couldn't believe it. It was the shortest shift yet! I had some time to relax. I hadn't checked my emails in a long while so decided to take a short trip to the internet café that was down the road.

I needed to hear good news. I was sick was living in the dark full of doom and gloom. I was excited to see that I had received an email from my friend Shamim. She had heard about my situation and was very concerned. She was a bearer of good news.

She wrote that she knew of someone that was visiting Dubai. She had very kindly spoken to him about me and asked him to meet up with me to give me some moral support. I was so relieved to hear this. It was crazy trying to deal with this on my own. Just the thought of having someone with me for support felt like I was finally moving in the right direction! She emailed me the number of this man who was called Azhar. I hadn't smiled that much in a long time. To be smiling again was a big achievement for me. I am eternally grateful to Shamim for her support.

It was nice to finally share some good news with Maher who was very happy for me. He had seen me at my worst and he had noticed the difference in me on this particular day. I went to bed early as I still had to go to the police station the following day.

The same walk the same everything, day in day out! It was tiresome! The previous day was a one off special in terms of timing and being seen earlier and having part of the day to myself. I must have waited a good three hours and there in front of me was Faizel. It was shock after shock. He was equally surprised to see me. He was very calm, all things considered. He sat beside me and for the millionth time I had to run through the situation. I was so apologetic to him. He was very understanding and it was so unfortunate that he was pulled in for questioning. He went in to the little room but wasn't in for too long. He said he didn't get grilled too heavily. I carried on with my apologies as I felt so bad for him. He was a kind person and was understanding of the ordeal I was going through. He wished me all the best with everything and went. That was the last time I would be seeing him!

It was now my turn to enter what felt like my living room at home. I seemed to be liaising with the same officer which made my life easier. What I heard next brought music to my ears. They would finally be issuing me with the statement stating that I had my passport stolen but I first needed to go to about three different government official offices to sign forms and get a stamped document to bring to the police station. There was always a *but*, however this but didn't seem too harsh or impossible. I felt a streak of excitement run through my body. I was finally making progress. The officer issued me with a letter that I would have to show to the staff at the different government offices in order for them to give me the appropriate forms to fill in. The day got even better.

I was able to leave early and I didn't have to come back to that depressing mind-numbing place until I had all the documents. Praise the Lord!

I managed to retain that smile on my face throughout my journey home. It was about time that things were on the up. I still wasn't too comfortable about wandering off aimlessly. My confidence was not the same as before. I used to love walking around by myself. Those days had gone. My walks just led me to the police station and back. It was truly a God send that all the shops were in reach. I went to a bakery to get some meat pastries and cakes. It was the first day that I felt like eating properly. I got everything packed to take away for me and Maher. After eating very little as my stomach had shrunk and my eyes had done most of the eating, I decided to call Azhar, the gentleman my friend Shamim had connected me with, to enlighten him about my situation. He was a very chilled out person and a great listener. The plan was that we would meet in the morning not far from the British embassy, and then trek to the offices and try to battle it out all in one day! All being well and if everything went according to plan, I would be able to take the documents to the police station and then to the embassy so that I could get my new passport issued. I hung up the phone feeling much more positive.

My case officer from the embassy, Caroline had called me a few of times and left lots of messages. I kept forgetting to get back to her so I made a point of calling her up. She picked up and was relieved to hear from me. I updated her on my progress and she was delighted to hear that I was finally moving upwards. She said that she would look forward to seeing me soon. God, if only, I thought! At least I was moving into the next phase. It was still a long haul. I was finally making progress whether I wanted to believe it or not!

CHAPTER 16

Abrand-new day! I was able to appreciate the fresh air much more than ever. My body was still in recovery from the shock it had endured. It was a working progress. I could see a tall man waiting at the meeting point where I was meeting Azhar. I didn't want to make a fool out of myself by waving just in case it was not him. I did have a record of mistaking people for who I thought they were and them turning out to be people I had never met in my life. That was due to being a bit short sighted. That was a good enough reason surely! As I got closer he smiled and introduced himself. I was right for once!

It was nice that we had a great connection, my friend Shamim. It all went from there. I was learning the art of summarising my story as it was draining having to go into detail every time and not to forget painful. I thanked him hugely for taking the time out of his schedule to accompany me on my mission. Along with the letter from the police I had been given the addresses of the offices I needed to go to. To be honest, I had no idea what these offices did or were. It was good to know they were situated within reasonable distance of each other.

So, office one! I showed my letter and we were then directed to another area where I had to take a ticket and wait in the waiting area. The massive room was split into different sections. It felt like waiting to be executed. It took ages. I was so grateful to have Azhar's company. He was very patient, more so than me! My number was called two hours later. I flashed the letter again and I was told to fill out certain parts of the form with basic information such as my name, UK address etc; the rest they would do themselves, which was worrying. It was of course all in Arabic. I was really at their mercy because in effect I could be signing my life away and would not even have a clue! All filled out and ready to trek to a different part of the hall. No sitting down here. We had to queue like we were queuing for school dinners. It was moving swiftly. They looked at my letter again and the form I had just partly filled out. The man stamped it! Hooray, my first stamp. One down two to go.

The next office was about fifteen minutes away. The sun was quite intense. We talked about life in the UK and how much I would appreciate every tiny little thing once back there. When asked if I would like to come back my answer was a straight 'no' without any hesitation. I was put off for life. I wanted to put all this behind me and try and forget it as if it were just a nightmare and not in fact reality.

The conversation was beginning to get a bit more serious and I didn't want that so I started talking about food, a subject we all like to talk about even though my appetite was unbelievably low. We arrived at our second destination; another dull and gloomy building from the inside. The procedure was very similar. We ploughed through the queues and went to the relevant desks. Another stamp! Just one more and that would be it! It didn't feel final in any way. I didn't think the realisation would kick in until I would be sitting on my seat in the aeroplane. It would be at that point that it would begin to feel more real!

The third and final stop! As we entered the building, we were hit with the body heat. It was jam packed. My face dropped. I just wished that this whole process was much simpler. It would take away a huge extra load of the stress. I had hoped that I would have had all the paperwork earlier that day so that I could have gone to the embassy to get my new passport. There was no way that was going to happen so I had to reluctantly erase that thought out of my head. Where to start, that was the question! I had to ask one of the staff members and he directed me to the receptionist. It was like being at a fish market. There simply was no room to breathe. After waiting in line just to get a ticket number we managed to find two seats that were hidden away discreetly. I was much less chatty now. My head was completely cluttered with a horrific amount of thoughts. What if they didn't stamp my document? This thought kept running through my mind. I was so used to disappointment. I needed to pick myself up and get back on the road to positivity.

It was going to be a long wait and there was nothing worse than sitting in silence especially when you had company so I instigated the conversation and as before we were both in full flow. Time passed much quicker and before we knew it my number was called. I had to get in line for some more stamping action whilst Azher remained seated. The form was short and sweet. The office worker just marked the questions I needed to fill in. Again it just basic information that was required which he explained. This time they wanted to take a thumb print so I stuck my right thumb on the ink pad then marked the document that required my print. It was really busy and noisy, but efficient. It was the best production line I had seen. The man finally stamped my last document. I wanted to scream in excitement but managed to contain myself. I thanked him and headed towards where Azhar was sitting. He saw the change of expression on my face and was equally happy for me. I walked out feeling a huge sense of relief! We walked a further few yards enough for the building to be a bit of a distance away. It was time for Azhar and me to say our goodbyes. I felt very sad.

He had been my tower of support through such a difficult time. We shook hands and then I hugged him and thanked him again and again.

My next and final stop of the day was to be to the police station for the very last time *inshallah*! (God willing)! The nerves started to kick in as I got closer to the police station. I loathed that place with a vengeance. I had spent more than my fair share of time in there. I walked in and was recognised straight away. To my disbelief I was fast tracked to the officer who was dealing with my case. Back into the little room for the last time! The officer was being very hospitable and asked me if I would like a drink. I agreed to some tea as I wasn't too sure how long this would take. I produced my requested documents, all stamped and ready to be traded in for a ticket to my freedom. He went through the documents like a tooth comb. He pulled out the letter from his drawer which was all ready for me but just needed to be stamped. He flicked through it carefully. As he was quite absorbed in reading the letter, my tea came. It was much needed and I knocked it back like a shot! The officer seemed satisfied with what he had read and so stamped my letter. The feeling I had at that moment was indescribable. I couldn't believe that I had got this far.

I was getting closer to getting out of what I considered hell at the time. He handed the letter over to me and wished me well. I thanked him and left. I couldn't have got out of there fast enough. The thought that I would never have to see that vile place again was as good to me as winning the lottery!

I got home and Maher was still out. It had been the longest day of my life. I didn't want it to be any longer and so fell asleep straight away.

It's true to say that was the best sleep I had in a very long time. It wasn't much but still. I was up bright and early ready for my last official stop at the embassy. I called Caroline to say that I was on my way. The tiredness of everything was beginning to kick in fast. I was completely worn out. I got to the embassy and waited in the waiting area. It wasn't long before Caroline came out. She was genuinely so happy to see me. We briefly chatted about how I had been. She could tell that I still wasn't in the best of ways but there was light ahead. I handed over the letter from the police and she immediately started with the process of getting me a new passport sorted. She said that it would cost in the region of about £200. As far as I was concerned it was the best spent money ever! I also needed some passport photos. There was a photographer's studio that I used to pass every day. I got up and headed out to get my photographs done. Normally I would jump at the chance of being in front of the camera.

That was my job, but this time the thought of being in front of a camera terrified me! I had lost all my confidence. I didn't want to see myself. I couldn't bear it!

Luckily for me it was really quiet at the studio so there was no waiting around. Just was a quick snapshot and done. The photographer asked me if I wanted to look at the photographs. I said that if he thought they were ok then I was happy with that. He put them in an envelope and I headed back to the embassy. It felt like it took me ages to get there. My speed was the pace of an old man. I strolled in and Caroline was there waiting for me. She said that it could take a couple of hours. I said that was fine and that I was happy to hang around there. I wasn't in the mood for walking around.

I waited in the waiting area. There was a stack of magazines. I must have flicked through every single one. After all, I did have enough time to kill. Flicking through all those magazines had tired me out and so I nodded off for a few moments.

I woke up two hours later. I went to the wash room to wake myself up. I washed my face with cold water. It seemed to have done the trick. I was alive again, well a bit more than before. As I walked out of the wash room, Caroline was seated in the waiting area waiting for me. She handed over to me my new passport. I was no longer an illegal immigrant. I could now officially book my ticket and head home to the UK. It was truly a miracle. As I flicked through I saw my photograph. I looked unrecognisable as my cheekbones were standing out abnormally. My face looked half the size. My hair wasn't as neat as it normally was. The most disturbing thing was my facial expression. It told such a sad story. My heart sank. My life had changed so drastically. I was no longer the happy go lucky person who loved and enjoyed life. It was devastating to digest. I closed the passport and put it in my bag. I gave Caroline a big tight hug and thanked her for all her support. She said to keep in touch. I said that I would once I was settled back in the UK. If nothing else I had a passport now and there was no way on God's earth that I would ever be parting with it!

The next task would be far more enjoyable. I needed to book my flight back home. I went to the nearest travel agent and asked when the next flight would be to the UK. I was happy to leave that same night but unfortunately that would not be possible. However there was a flight the following evening which would get me back into Manchester for about 8am. I was more than happy.

Without wasting any more time, I paid for the ticket. The agent gave me all my required documents and I left feeling a bit more optimistic. I had just over a day to get everything together.

It had been a long day and all I wanted to do was go back to the flat and relax. I had most certainly over exerted myself.

As soon as I got in I headed to bed. It was nice and snug. Three hours later I was up and feeling a little better. The sleep most definitely helped. I forced myself up and got changed. I wanted to share the good news with everyone so I called up my mum first. I was elated that after such a long time I could give her some good news. She was ecstatic. I hadn't spoken to my grandmother in a long time. I intentionally avoided speaking to her because I knew how heart-broken she would be and it would hurt me equally to know that she was upset especially because of me. I felt it would be better to speak to her face to face.

The news spread around like wild fire and it was nice to know that everyone was awaiting my arrival. I wanted to let my friends know of the good news too so I went to the internet café. I sent emails to Shahin and Shamim. I also had an interesting email from a client that I had worked for some time ago. The client was not aware that I had even been out of the country. There was a catwalk show happening and I was needed to model in the show. Without thinking whatsoever, I replied back to the client to say that I would be more than happy to take part in the show that was taking place a few days later. I didn't spend too much time in the net café and so went back to the flat to sort my few bits out as my flight was the following evening.

Maher came back from work earlier as he was aware that I would be leaving but not sure how soon. I broke the news that I had booked my flight to go back. He was really happy for me. If it wasn't for him I would have been on the streets of Dubai, penniless and homeless! I could tell that he was sad that I would be going as he enjoyed my company even though I wasn't in the best of ways. He had got used to me being around.

It took very little time to get my packing done as there was hardly anything to pack. I had spent the money sent to me very wisely. I had to invest in a couple of new outfits that were cheap basics. For now, they were fine. It was decided that we would eat out as it was my last night in Dubai. I was happy with that. We opted for the local café that served some nice Arabic food. Again, I didn't eat much. I forced down as much as I could. It was well made home cooked style food.

It was such a pleasant evening full of light-hearted conversations and chilling out. I was finally calming down enough to be able to enjoy the moment the best I could.

We got in later than expected. Maher went straight to bed whilst I gathered my things and put them in my travel bag. Feeling more satisfied, I went to bed.

I had set my alarm early so I could say my goodbyes to Maher as he would be working till late which meant that I would not see him. He was all dressed and ready for work. I quickly brushed my teeth and put the kettle on for tea. It was another emotional good bye because Maher had truly been an angel in disguise. If it wasn't for him I would have been in more of a severe situation. I thanked him with all my heart and promised to keep in touch. I had made a friend for life. He said to let him know when I got home. My emotions got the better of me and so the tears flooded my face. I had become an emotional wreck and would cry at almost everything. Maher had really saved me! We hugged and Maher headed to work whilst I got back to making my tea.

It was a surreal feeling because finally I was going to be free from all this hell for good. It was beginning to feel like a dream that was too good to be true and that any minute I would be hit with the harsh realities! The thing is, it was all for real! With that thought I drank my tea whilst watching television escaping anymore negative thoughts. I needed to be at the airport for 6pm sharp. It was best to leave about 4.30pm due to crazy traffic even though the journey wasn't too long.

The few hours passed quickly. I was all ready for leaving Dubai. I grabbed my luggage, gave a once over look to the flat and said good bye. I locked the door and posted the keys that Maher had cut for me through the letter box. All that was left now was to grab a taxi from outside to take me to the airport and nothing else!

CHAPTER 17

There was never a shortage of taxis that was for sure. I had just put my bag down when one stopped right in front of me. I got in and threw my bag to the other side of the back seat. Normally I would be chatting away to the driver, having a giggle but I didn't have the energy. The traffic was very much stop and start. I gazed through the window to take a final glimpse of the city that I once loved dearly. I was glad to see the signs for the airport which were visible now. Not long to go, I kept thinking to myself. The driver parked up, I paid him and took my bag and walked into the airport. I don't know why but my nerves were beginning to get the better of me. I paused, took a deep breath then headed towards check in. The counters had just opened. There were not many people in the queue. I checked in without any problems. Going through security was a breeze and then came immigration. There was a bit of a wait, as always. I was waiting in line, feeling really nervous now, to the point where I could feel myself shaking uncontrollably. If I didn't get through immigration, I would forever be doomed in Dubai. My mind was working over-time. I kept taking deep breaths to calm myself down. It seemed to work eventually.

Only one person in front of me and then it was my turn at the desk.

The person in front of me went forward. My heart started to race again. The desk was vacant. I froze on the spot for what seemed like a good few seconds. The man behind the desk asked me to come forward for the second time. I didn't hear him the first time at all. He took my passport studied it for what seemed like a lifetime then he looked at me then back at the passport. Every second felt like an hour. If I didn't get through now then that would be the end of me for good! To my ultimate delight he stamped it and let me through. What a relief! I couldn't believe it. Miracles do happen. I was finally going home.

I managed to find a seat in the departure lounge, got comfortable and then decided to make a phone call home. My aunt picked up. She asked how I was. I just kept saying that I was finally coming home and how amazing that was. It's like I had to convince myself every few seconds that that was the truth. I still had that tiny bit of doubt in my voice. She said that everyone was really looking forward to seeing me and that how much I was missed. I didn't need to worry about anything as I would be met at the airport. I cut the conversation short because if I had carried on talking I would have flooded the place with my tears. I also sent Maher a text message with regards to my progress. He replied saying not to worry about anything and that I would be back on track in no time.

I really wanted to believe that! I was too damaged. I had become an emotional wreck and could not see that far into the future.

Everyone was getting up to board so I joined the queue. I looked forward and didn't look back. I wanted to leave all the negativity behind. The crew on board were very friendly. I managed to bag a window seat. The whole row was full; in fact it was a very busy flight. I was hoping that I would be able to sleep. My body and mind were overworked and overloaded and in desperate need of relaxation. Before long, dinner was served and I pecked at the food like a little bird. As usual I wasn't hungry. The only way I would get any sleep would be to watch films in the hope that would tire me out. It took two whole films to knock me out. I got up about forty minutes before landing. The flight had been comfortable. Just hearing the words that we would shortly be landing at Manchester Airport sounded extremely surreal! My head was still in a daze. I had yet to face another huge challenge and that was facing my family!

Finally, we touched down on UK soil. I was in no hurry to get out and so let everyone go first. I casually walked down the aisle, thanked the crew for the good service and headed towards baggage reclaim. I felt like I was in a dream. It was the strangest feeling ever. It felt like I had been away for years and not several months. I was feeling quite alienated.

Again, in no major hurry, I went to get my bag. I didn't have to wait at all as I had just spotted it coming on the carousel. I ran as fast as I could, which wasn't very fast. I grabbed it and headed towards the nothing to declare exit. My heart started up again. I needed to be composed, at least for now. That walk to the final exit doors must have been the slowest walk in history. The shakes started up again. I was a complete mess. As I walked I started to take deep breaths and pull myself together.

I couldn't see any familiar faces. Suddenly, there right at the bottom left was a little congregation of my family members. They looked both happy and sad, mingled with shock. They couldn't believe how much weight I had lost. My grandmother was the first person I hugged. I couldn't control my emotions and started crying like a baby. We hugged for ages and then I moved along the line to my mum and then my aunt. I really tried to keep my feelings aside but it was impossible. We all had a good cry and then headed towards the car park.

I still was in dreamland. I felt that any moment I would wake up and start re-living my nightmare. It took a good while for me to come to terms with the fact that I had finally reached the UK.

We all got into the car. I wanted to sit at the back. There was the most awkward silence for a while which I broke by asking how everyone else was. I couldn't wait to see my cousins and nephew. It was nice to have a few moments of normality. The roads were nice and clear that time of the morning and we got home in good time. My car was still parked up outside in its usual spot. The whole street looked like it hadn't changed in any way shape or form. I walked inside the house. I sat down in my normal seat. It felt great and so comfortable. I wanted to go to bed and feel fresh for when I saw my sister and everyone later.

I hugged everyone then headed to my room which looked untouched. I was finally back. When was this going to sink in? I had to take each step at a time. I got into my pyjamas and fell fast asleep in my comfortable bed. I fell into a deep sleep and before long I was back in my apartment in Dubai making dinner feeling overjoyed with my cooking. Then the door bursts open and the gang of four men come in each holding a weapon. The main guy has a knife in his hand whilst the others are holding baseball bats in their hands. I dropped the plate of food and started screaming, saying 'I haven't done anything why are you here'?

The main man screams, 'Why are you lying to us. Give me the money'. I am shouting in a terrified tone that I don't have the money Luca does. Not believing a word the man with the knife grabs me by the neck and stabs me in the stomach. I am screaming in agony for help but no one hears me then the men with the bats start to beat me. I woke up screaming and crying hysterically. I had a very real nightmare. I got up feeling very stressed. I was sweating a lot too. My mum came running up to my room to see if I was ok. I clearly wasn't. She hugged me and then I went downstairs with her.

My favourite dishes had been cooked. I forced myself to eat more than normal just to please my grandmother. She spent so much time cooking with love. I didn't want to hurt her feelings. There was so much I needed to do. I needed to contact my UK network provider so that at least I would be contactable. My phone from Dubai was unlocked so I could put any SIM card in there. After lunch, I asked my mum to make me some tea whilst I called up my network provider from the home phone to send me a SIM card. I explained to them that I had my phone stolen and so on. They were quite forth coming and agreed to get the SIM card to me next day.

I wasn't in the mood for doing anything and so spent the rest of the day watching television. I didn't speak much to anyone, however everyone respected that. The day went by peacefully. I went to bed early hoping that I would get some rest but unfortunately that was not the case. I had the same dream again. It was driving me insane. I didn't dare close my eyes because I feared that I would be transported back to the hell on earth that I was living in. This was very unhealthy because I started to think too much. I went deep into myself and read into things on a completely different level. I felt like I was going totally insane. I must have managed about an hour's sleep maximum.

The sun was shining through the gap of where the curtains met and I went down to see if my SIM card had come and as promised it was there. I had starting to build up a few of my contacts. My friends emailed me their numbers and then stored them onto my new phone.

I text messaged Shamim, Amar and Shahin to say that I had arrived home. They replied to say how happy and relieved they were to hear that. Shahin mentioned that she would be performing locally to me over the weekend and that I should try to come to see her. It seemed like a great idea as I needed a diversion. I wanted to get back to normal as soon as possible. I hated the idea of being stuck inside. I had done enough of that abroad.

I was desperate to see my sister and my nephew. Unfortunately, I still hadn't seen her. She had been very busy and wanted me to rest up. I wanted to walk to her house as it was only a short journey, besides the fresh air would do me a world of good! I got dressed in whatever I could find. This was extremely unusual for me as I used to be so picky and particular about how I put outfits together. I was just happy with what I found. The strange feeling was still within me but I had to try and put it aside. I enjoyed the warm breeze. It wasn't as hot as Dubai or as harsh.

I got there in exactly ten minutes and knocked at the door. My sister opened it. I was proud of myself for holding back the tears. She was emotional of course and could not believe the state I was in. I looked stick thin. My beautiful nephew looked much bigger. I grabbed him and hugged him tight. He was my bundle of joy. He always made me forget my worries. We chatted for some time. I really valued these priceless moments. I needed to check my emails as the client that I had agreed to do the catwalk show for was going to send me details of the show. I did indeed get the email and it stated that I would need to attend a rehearsal the following day.

I replied to say that I would be there. After sending the email I wondered to myself whether I was doing the right thing by jumping into the deep end by doing a job. I couldn't even look at myself in a mirror, so how could I walk down a catwalk with lots of people looking at me?

I wanted normality back and so convinced myself that this would be a great step forward into achieving that. My sister tried to feed me. I couldn't fit anything more in. My stomach had shrunk hugely and so I was only able to eat very small portions.

I left her house and walked back home. I decided to call Shahin on the way who was naturally very concerned. She was ecstatic to hear my voice. I said that I would bring my mum and grandmother to the Mela which is an annual cultural festival that features Asian food, fashion and music. Shahin was going to be performing my favourite tracks. I was looking forward to the event. Before going to Dubai I had also done a lot of event management work and so formed a great team of models, designers, hair & makeup artists. We used to get booked to do all the shows. Not only did I manage the team, I put together the whole fashion show as well model on the catwalk. I loved my work. This would be the first time I would be attending an event where I wasn't involved. No doubt it was going to feel very strange.

The days were rolling into one. I had completely lost track of the days. The day of the fashion show rehearsal had arrived. It was in Bolton which was about a thirty-minute drive. I was nervous about driving because I hadn't driven in ages. The thing with driving is it's a skill that's never forgotten. I dressed very modestly and took my portfolios with me. It was a nice sunny day for a drive. My mum and grand-mother were a bit concerned about me behind the wheel. I assured them that I would be fine. The thing was I didn't have a single penny on me. I had lost every penny I owned. There was no petrol in the car. I felt blessed because I didn't even have to say anything. My grandmother was totally understanding of my situation as she insisted on giving me some money. I felt very ashamed of accepting this very kind gesture as by rights it should be me giving money to her. I hated myself for taking it but I didn't have a choice.

I filled up my car and headed to the venue. It was quite a therapeutic short drive. I didn't drive to the best of my ability but I was safe and got there in one piece. I parked up in the allocated parking space and went inside. The rehearsals were taking place in the actual venue of where the show was going to be held.

It was a beautiful hotel with such intricate detail everywhere you looked. The client saw me as I walked in and was really pleased that I had agreed to do the show. I had to try on some clothes to ensure that they had got my sizes right. They always seem to get my sizes wrong for some strange reason.

There was one time where I was doing some shows for a mall and they misprinted my name to Nadine and assumed I was female so when I turned up on the day of the show, they had an amazing range of girlie teenage outfits for me. I was initially really annoyed about their ignorance but then laughed it off like a true professional. The clothes that were picked for me on this occasion were very tasteful and fitted reasonably well apart from one outfit where the jacket was way too big for my frame. They said they would replace it. It was all good. Everyone in the team seemed very nice and level headed.

It was time for a short break and then we would have to go through our positions on the catwalk. This put me into panic mode. I didn't feel confident walking. I kept trying to reason with myself but it wasn't happening. The thought of walking on the stage with all these eyes glaring at me freaked me out.

What was I thinking? I wasn't ready for all this, it was way too early. The more I thought about it the more it made sense that I should not be there. I had to make an excuse and leave immediately. I said to the client that I needed to leave for another casting. He was completely fine with that as he knew that I was a very experienced model with a very strong walk. I managed to get out of that one reasonably well. I was trying too hard to overcome my horrific experience by side tracking myself with anything I could grab hold of. It wasn't working. I needed to let things progress naturally. I wasn't ready to face the world just yet!

CHAPTER 18

The sun may have been shining but I was sinking deeper within myself every day. I had sent a text to the client regarding the fashion show. I said that I wasn't well. I had never used that excuse ever in my working life. It was true and that was the sad thing.

It was the day of Shahin's performance. I was reluctant to get out of bed but I had made a promise to support her and would see it through! Even the tiniest of things were a huge effort. The nightmares continued day in day out. The bags under my eyes were literally down to my knees. I looked and felt very rough. I avoided all mirrors at all times, but by accident saw myself in the mirror in the hallway. I was unrecognisable to myself! I could not believe what I saw. The shock hit deep.

I was so happy to take my grandmother and mum to the festival. It would be a nice day out for them and at least it was getting me out of the house too.

The drive was short and sweet and we managed to get good parking right outside the venue which was perfect as I didn't want my mum and grandmother to have a trek walking. As I entered the park, it brought back all the memories of when I used to be involved in the festivals. The atmosphere was vibrant. I got a couple of chairs for my mum and grandmother then headed backstage where Shahin was getting ready for her performance. On my way to the marquee I saw so many familiar faces which were a pleasant surprise for me. It was no problem getting backstage as my old friends were involved with the event and were more than happy to let me through.

There she was, all ready to do her stuff on stage. The last time I saw her was in Dubai and she wasn't really sure what had happened. I hadn't been able to speak to her in more depth and it obviously would not be possible at that moment. Shahin looked amazing in her fusion blingy outfit. The crowds were certainly ready for her. When she went on stage the crowds went crazy. She had a live percussionist playing the darbouka which is an Arabic drum with such beautiful versatile sounds. I started to get goose pimples as I always did when she performed. For those few moments, I was far away from all my troubles. It was an amazing feeling. The performance was spectacular and drawing to an end. I was ready to go home and hit club duvet. My duvet was my biggest comfort. I hugged Shahin and promised to call her soon for an in depth chat. My mum and grandmother had enjoyed their day out too which made me happy.

The journey home was quiet. Just a few words here and there, nothing more! As soon as we got home, I ran upstairs to my room. I didn't want to be disturbed. I needed space. Some of my family were coming over for a short visit from the midlands. I wasn't in a hosting mood. I was not going to force myself to do anything for anyone.

I tried my best to get some sleep but sleep had not befriended me. As always I was tired and feeling lethargic. It was a case of trying to get through each day with as much ease as possible which was not easy on any account. A few hours later I could hear many voices. The living room was directly under my room. My family had come. I thought it best to go down and say 'hi', get it over with and then head back upstairs. I was very slow going down the stairs. The room was crowded with people. I didn't know where to look and the sound was making me dizzy. I sat down for a few seconds, got up and then went to say my hellos. It was too overwhelming for me.

Mostly everyone asked if I was ok. I lied and said I was fine. It was easier to say that. Then one of my uncles through marriage was trying to make conversations just to have his cheap digs at me and to have the satisfaction of saying, 'well I told you so'. Told me what? I was beginning to feel angry. He was referring to the fact that I had gone to Dubai but had to come back to the UK because I had failed. I was so disgusted. He hadn't told me anything. No one really knew the truth of what had really happened as I had kept it brief by saying that my passport was stolen and I had met some nasty people who had lied to me, promised me a job and taken all my money. They didn't know the half of it! How dare anybody kick me down when I was already at my lowest point! I am glad that I didn't say much more than this because, of course, it would have been my fault that I had been battered and bruised and that I had been sexually assaulted! I had heard enough and went back to my room.

I was feeling dirty all over again and blaming myself for what had happened. How could I have been so naïve and not seen a single sign of what was to come? I should have resisted more when I was being abused even though it was not physically possible at all. The thoughts were driving me insane. The stress of it all was getting the best of me. By now I had no confidence whatsoever. I had no contact with the outside world. My mobile phone was always switched off. Someone would come up to me at regular times to make sure that I was ok. I only went downstairs to eat once a day. That was my everyday life in a nutshell.

The days were passing and I was going from bad to worse. I hated myself more each day. I was sick of everything, everyone. How could I have let my family down? All I did was let everybody down, including me!

I hated life! What did I have to live for? Nothing! What was the point? Nobody would care if I wasn't around, anyway. I needed out of this situation once and for all. I needed to put myself out of my misery. I had nothing to my name. No money, no career, nothing! I had to rebuild my life from scratch! I didn't have the energy. How would people react if they found out that I had been raped? I would be hated even more. I couldn't do it to myself or my family. I didn't want to live anymore. I had nothing to live for. It would be the best thing for me and everyone else if I ended it!

The more I thought about it the more sense it made. At least I would be at peace forever and I wouldn't need to answer to anyone. The idea was becoming so appealing that I got up and went to my medicine drawer. I had an unopened box of paracetamols. I took the box and emptied out the packets which held the tablets. I took a deep sigh, tears rolling heavily down my cheeks. It was the right decision. I wanted to be free from everything. The thought of being completely free was enough for me to start knocking back the tablets one by one in my mouth and then bang, I was out!

I woke up completely dazed and confused. I didn't know where I was. My vision was blurry and I couldn't make heads or tails of anything. Slowly, slowly my vision was becoming clearer. I could see the devastated faces of my sister and mum. They were distraught but relieved that I had come around. I had no idea what had happened. I didn't know if it was for real or whether I was in another dimension as I was seeing the light! My eyes closed and I was knocked out again.

I woke up after what seemed like days. I was more alert now but frustrated that I could not remember exactly what had happened to me. I was aware that I was in hospital. My family had been at my bedside for a ridiculous number of hours. Still a bit dazed I asked my sister what had happened. She seemed reluctant to tell me but I insisted she did. She said everyone was downstairs talking and relaxing then they all heard the biggest bang coming from my room. I had rolled over and fallen onto the floor. The sound was evidently magnified because of my dead weight as I had passed out well and truly. They had seen the tablets, put two and two together and called for an ambulance straight away. My stomach had to be pumped as they were unsure as to how many tablets I had taken. I couldn't believe what I was hearing. I felt so guilty for putting my family through this. It had torn them in two. I didn't have a choice at that moment in time. I had hit rock bottom. It was quite a tense and fragile atmosphere and there was no way on God's earth that I would reveal all the finer details of what happened in Dubai to anyone else. They assured me that they would always be there for me no matter what which helped. It was time for me to rest up and wait for the doctor to do his rounds. I insisted that my sister and everyone should go home and get some rest. They needed assurance from me that I wasn't going to do anything silly. There wasn't much chance of that being in a hospital.

Getting hold of a nurse was difficult enough let alone any medication to overdose myself on! I promised that they should not worry and that I would need their support once I was out of hospital. It was comforting for them to know that I had acknowledged the fact that I needed them and that I had openly asked for their support. I did still feel very unsettled, depressed and totally confused with myself. It was a horrific feeling of being neither here nor there. I needed to get to grips with what was going on and take it from there.

The doctor eventually came and I was feeling much more alert. The first question I asked was when I could go home. I hated hospitals and that horrible smell that always lingered. He said I needed to get as much rest as possible and that I would be out of there once I got my strength back as I was evidently very weak and frail. He checked my blood pressure and heart beat. Thankfully everything was in working order however my blood pressure was a bit high. No surprise really! He also stated that I was very lucky to be alive as if the ambulance had not come when it did, it would have been fatal. Basically, I would have died! This sent huge shivers down my spine. The reality of death was in my face which made me realise that death was not the answer to my situation. The doctor had finished and I was feeling tired so I went back to sleep.

A few days passed by with me resting up and trying to build my strength back. My sister would bring some lovely home cooked food which was great as I was slowly beginning to get my appetite back. There was a huge concern about my mental health as that was the reason for me being in hospital in the first place. The doctors had recommended that I have a word with the psychiatrist once I was feeling better. I didn't argue with this. I needed to let it all out. It was too much to keep it bubbling inside. My health seemed to be on the up as I had been injected with glucose which gave me energy. Physically I was looking better and feeling better which was amazing. It was what was lurking in my head that needed some attention.

I was sat up on my bed watching day time trashy television when a nurse came to take me to my appointment with the psychiatrist. She had my mean machine at the ready, a very cool looking wheelchair. She was a lovely young stunning looking nurse with a great sense of humour. We got on famously.

She took me inside the room where I would be having a one to one chat with the psychiatrist. The reality of why I was there was beginning to freak me out. I had barely come to terms with the fact that I had taken an overdose and that I was in hospital, the place I hated the most. Even so, I knew it would be helpful to talk to a stranger. I couldn't speak to my family in detail, or anyone else for that matter. I needed to be sensible about this situation. I couldn't carry on feeling sorry for myself. Thinking about it, I had made a stupid decision in taking the tablets. It was a cowardly thing to do and I felt that I had been given a second chance in life. I needed to grasp it with both hands and appreciate it. It was easier said than done.

The psychiatrist walked in. He looked like he was in his early thirties, average height with dark features. He introduced himself as Darren. I was feeling uncomfortable all over again. I had to fight my demons. I used to be a very strong person and I would be a strong person again but I needed to push myself more and more to achieve that. He spoke very softly and asked me how I was feeling. I needed to be honest and say it how it was no matter how difficult it would be. Besides he wasn't there to judge me. He kept assuring me that whatever we discussed would be just between me and him. I had issues with trust hugely because it was due to trust that I landed in such a big mess. He was a professional and there to better me. That's what I kept reminding myself of. I needed to risk giving a bit of trust.

Right, where to start? This wasn't going to be easy by any means. I took a deep breath then very slowly began to open up. As I retold my story, my emotions were getting the better of me to the point where I was crying non-stop. He said it was good to let it out. It was an opportunity to off load everything that had been building up inside and driving me crazy. Darren offered me some tissues. I tidied myself up and continued with my story.

When I finally arrived at the point I most dreaded, I braced myself and told him everything, right down to the finest detail. Darren's face was quite a picture of both shock and sympathy. He listened, giving me his full attention. It was all beginning to make full sense to him. I assured him that what I had done in terms of taking the tablets was completely out of character for me. I had been a completely confident person before this nightmare. I had known exactly what I wanted from life.

It felt so therapeutic off loading. I felt lighter. The session had been very productive. He then asked me how I felt about life. I paused and then said I had learned that what I did was wrong but felt I couldn't handle the pressure at that moment in time. Everything had got the better of me and I had lost complete control of my life! I now felt that I had a new lease of life and that I would never ever even consider ending it again. Life was a gift that needed to be treasured. I had too much to lose like my immediate family. There was no reason that I could not be a model again.

I needed to work on my confidence and get to the point in life where I would be able to take control of it again. It was not impossible!

It wasn't going to happen overnight but it was going to happen for sure. Darren did assure me. It was nice to have that normal feeling however the subject of the conversation began to take a complete different turn. Coming back down to earth, Darren as politely as he could be mentioned the fact that I would need to have a HIV test and that he would speak to the doctor about it and get it arranged. This made me quiver in my seat and made me feel so unclean and disgraceful. It was not what I wanted to hear but it was something that needed attention whether I liked it or not. The session was positive one but it also had a taste of the harsh reality that I was living in. I was taken back to the ward by another nurse, not the one I had befriended. There weren't too many people on the ward but a mere few ranging from twenty years old to seventy. I kept myself to myself.

I was having regular sessions with Darren and making great progress. He kept his word and arranged for me to take the HIV test. I felt so degraded but it was a must. They would notify me of the results via post in a few days. I needed to forget about that for a while and worry about the immediate moment. Being a born worrier made it extremely difficult!

Finally, the day that I had been daydreaming of had arrived. I was being discharged from the hospital. Being in hospital had given me some good thinking time. I could re-evaluate my situation more comfortably. I seemed to be blessed with some inner strength which made me very proud of myself. I had learnt that life was indeed very precious. It was now up to me to make of it what I would. I could either forever be negative or stew in the past or I could build myself up and make something of my life. I was well enough now to understand that I needed to get myself out of this rut, pull myself together, build on my confidence and start pushing my career again. Who cared if I had to build my life from scratch at the age of thirty? There were people around the world in much more worse situations. A lot of people were not fortunate like me to have a second chance but I did, and I was going to embrace it fully!

My sister picked me up and I went home feeling more positive than ever. Everyone was amazed at how much progress I had made. The signs of the normal me were becoming a bit more evident. It was so great to be welcomed home with so much love and care. Everyone had gone through so much effort to make my return home so special, the massive spread on the table, banners, balloons, and the beautiful vibrant atmosphere. However, the guilty feeling of having put everyone through what I did still lingered.

I, like everyone else am human. Everyone makes mistakes. If we were all prim and perfect, we would not be human but angels. There were no more discussions of my soul-destroying situation which I was so glad of.

I wanted it to be a thing of the past. Naturally it would take time for the wounds to heal. I needed to be strong and keep my focus on positive things like getting my health back on track and getting back on the catwalk. The main thing was, I was on the mend which was all that mattered. I felt like a new person and ready to take on the world no matter what would be thrown at me!

CHAPTER 19

The weeks were passing as quickly as if they were days; less painfully. I wasn't spending as much time in my room as before, to my family's relief. I even managed to start getting changed out of my pyjamas into normal clothing which was a big break through. A couple of times I had looked in the mirror by mistake and not jumped out of my skin. It was happening gradually, slowly but surely. One day I asked for food without being forced which stunned my grandmother. I ate it with pleasure. I felt different inside. It's such a true saying that once you have hit rock bottom the only way is up. I would have refused to believe this at one point in my life however I was living proof that this was true!

It was a beautiful sunny day and I wanted to be outdoors. I was sitting on a chair in the front garden absorbing the rays of sunshine. It was around mid-morning and the postman was delivering the afternoon post. I stood up to get the mail from him. He greeted me with a smile and handed over the letters. There were two letters addressed to me and one to my grand-mother. I was suddenly back in panic mode! I became very paranoid and on edge which triggered off my nerves to another level. I hadn't had much mail for a long time and was curious to know what had come through. I was expecting a specific letter from the hospital but that was it. I put my grandmother's letter on the side board and ran upstairs to my room. My anxiety was in full swing. My hands were shaking like a leaf as I tried to open one of the envelopes. The letters 'NHS' was boldly plastered on the front. It was going to be either good news or not, simple as. I had no control of the situation. All I could do now was open the letter and put myself out of my misery!

As I fumbled with the envelope, I seemed to freeze on the spot. No matter how much I tried to unfold the paper, my hands refused to move. I took a deep breath, paused for a moment and went for it. As I read the letter, my concern and worries melted away. It was fantastic news. I was in the clear. It was unbelievable, but I had to believe it because it was written crystal clear in black and white. I shouted 'yes' so loud that my mum came running up to see if I was ok. She was hugely relieved to see me smiling; something I hadn't been able to do for a very long time. One down, one to go! Who was the other letter from? I had had the best news and nothing else could bring me down. I opened the letter with great curiosity. It was from one of my model agents writing to me saying that I had received some royalties from a shoot that I had done a year ago. The client wanted to re-use my photograph for another year.

Along with the slip was a cheque of £400 made out to me for doing absolutely nothing. How amazing? This second bit of good news completely changed my mood. I was feeling happy from within. It was a beautiful feeling. I had craved this for so long. My confidence was on the up for sure. The trick now was to keep on this level and not lose focus.

I had finally befriended the mirror and was able to look at myself without being hypocritical and going into deep analysis.

I was putting on some weight in the right places. My frame was healthier than the extreme skinny starved look I had previously. I wanted to get out and about; appreciate my life. There had been too much time wasted. I had a lot of catching up to do. It was nice to be able to go out without constantly looking over my shoulder and not feeling irritated by other people. I was feeling normal, a very precious feeling indeed. I was really missing work hugely and needed to reconnect with my agencies so I took a trip to the library and contacted all my model agencies and all the clients I had worked for previously to say that I was back from Dubai and ready to start working again. They didn't need to know any more than that.

A day after having sent the emails, the phone was ringing. My mother agency which is basically what they call what you consider to be your main agency called me to say that they had arranged a test shoot for me in Manchester. A test shoot is where a model works with the photographer to get a variation of looks for the model's portfolio. Having been out of the circuit for a long time, naturally my look had changed so it was important to get fresh material for my book. I was ecstatic. I needed this. I was booked to go to the studio within a couple of days. It was nice to be worrying about the shoot rather than mind screwing things. I told everyone about it. It was a huge step up for me. It was nice to share it with people that genuinely cared for my wellbeing. It was so amazing to see how happy everyone was for me. They were happy that I was now focusing on more positive things which would then lead me to the road of full recovery, all being well.

This would be my first shoot after a very, very long time. I was hoping that I still had it. I didn't want to disappoint anyone! I was working with a top photographer and didn't want to cut my chances of any future assignments that I could possibly get. I thought it a good idea to have a practise at home by simply posing in front of the mirror to warm up. There's nothing more frustrating than for a photographer having to work with a wooden model that is lifeless in front of the camera. I needed to remind myself that in the bigger scheme of things, to be fair, this was not my first shoot ever.

I had done hundreds of them and walked down endless catwalks. So, for a day and a half, I spent most of my time in front of the mirror. I felt much more relaxed and more confident. Only a day to go and then it would be show time.

I was organised as always and took everything with me except for the kitchen sink! I made sure that I had my hairsprays, makeup kit etc even though there would be a makeup artist on set. I had two model bags which had all the necessities needed for a shoot. One I had taken to Dubai and one that was still in my wardrobe. I packed some casual clothing as well as more formal attire in order to get contrasting looks.

I needed to be at the studio for 11am and so left home at 9am. I have a phobia of being late. I would much rather get there hours early than be a few minutes late. Even though I was more confident than before, my stomach was churning. I had to be professional and simply get on with it regardless of how I was feeling!

I got to the studio early. The photographer was all set up to go and so was the make-up artist. I opened my bag and hung up my collection of clothes on the clothing rail so both the photographer and makeup artist would have a clearer vision of the kind of theme we would be going for. Outfits all sorted, now time to take the hot seat to get my hair and makeup done. It was quite therapeutic as I sat there having interesting conversations with the make-up artist. It turned out that we had worked with a lot of the same models. Small world! She was a true professional as she had made me up in such a short space of time. I then got changed into my first outfit that they selected. As difficult as it was for me, I needed to put mind over matter. I couldn't afford to mess this up at any cost.

As always, I took a few deep breaths and headed towards the white backdrop. The spot lights were on and I was finding them abnormally bright. It was time to put everything behind me and work it like a professional. Initially I was a bit rusty and stiff but then suddenly I transformed into a completely different person. I was posing and pouting and going for it full pelt. I didn't care how uncomfortable I felt in the pose. I wanted some amazing images and I was working my hardest to get them. The more the photographer complimented me on my performance the more my confidence rose. I was in and out of outfits working like a true professional I had always been. I was so proud of myself. When I went to get changed into my normal clothes, I kept grinning to myself. I had completed this very dreaded mission. Both the photographer and makeup artist were so impressed with my performance and professionalism.

To see that kind of reaction was priceless for me. It was great to feel like a model again. As I left the studio I called the agency to give them feedback, as I always did with every job. There were times where I would work with clients that were very chilled out to the point where you could have a laugh with them but in contrast there were clients that were very hard-faced and extremely formal. In situations like this I would just do my work without saying much and go home. The agency was delighted that the shoot had gone well and was equally excited to see the results. I was told the turnaround would be quick as I needed to start work as soon as possible. I was officially ready to do my thing!

Late afternoon the following day, I got a call from my agency. The photographs had come through and they were more than happy with the results. They were going to keep the disc with the images on them for themselves and send me six prints. It was money well invested.

I impatiently checked the post in the morning. There was special delivery for me. I signed for it and ripped open the hardback envelope which said please do not bend as carefully as I could. They were definitely my prints. I pulled them out one by one. I was in utter shock. I couldn't believe it was me in the photographs. I looked like a high flying editorial model. It was the best feeling ever. All that hard work had paid off.

Within a couple of days the phone was ringing non-stop for work. I invested in a diary and noted down all the jobs that I was doing including who the clients were, what I was being paid, plus start and finish times just in case any overtime was due. I was so focused on my work. It was my sole priority and the reason for waking up in the morning.

I would love getting text messages from my friends saying that they had seen my photographs on posters, billboards in random places. It boosted me right up.

A couple of weeks later I was working in London in Hyde Park on a lifestyle shoot. It was a big job with a big team. I was meeting lots of interesting characters. One of the things I so loved about my work was meeting people from all walks of life. I had made some amazing friends this way. Every shoot was different and a completely different experience. Some more memorable than others! This was a stills shoot and we had just stopped for a break. There was a fantastic spread laid out for us. We had already had a big lunch. It was now tea time which meant tea, coffee and lots of delicious cakes. In between shots all we did was eat and eat.

For people that have this vision of models just eating lettuce leaves and cucumber, they couldn't be more wrong as all the models I have worked with have healthy appetites and would happily put up a fight for the last chocolate biscuit in the packet! Whilst stuffing my face with a gorgeous looking fresh strawberry tart topped with fresh cream which was screaming 'eat me', I felt my phone vibrate in my pocket. I tried to look dignified by wiping off all the cream off my face that had travelled all the way to my nose. All cleaned up and more respectable! Who was calling me? It was my agency. It was usually a good sign when they called. It was just a reminder to say that the film project that I had worked on a good few months before I had left for Dubai was about to be released. I had totally forgotten about that but then my head was overly occupied and fried.

The film also starred Om Puri and Sophie Dahl. The film was about a film and I landed the part of Priyesh, whose father buys him a role in a film. It was a real pleasure working with the whole team, most of who had flown out from Mumbai. Sophie Dahl is so stunning in real life and a lovely person. Om Puri was hugely inspiring. It was paramount that I make most of this opportunity in order to get as much exposure as possible. One of my friends was kind enough to send a press release on my behalf to all the media, including radio stations, magazines and newspapers. The response was tremendous. My mobile phone was ringing like a hotline number, non-stop! I was more than happy to go out there and talk about my experiences of working with A-Listers and the Bollywood crew. I even got asked to make appearances for various events. It was like being a celebrity! I loved every bit of it, I have to admit.

There was one particular event I was asked to make an appearance at. It was a fashion show where I had to go on stage and do a little speech. It was amazing just to be able to go on stage and speak confidently about myself. I felt like I had conquered the world. It was more about me and how far I had come and not me showing off and being stuck up! One of the main organisers was working on a project in the Middle East, the UAE to be more precise. They were making a colourful documentary about how contrasting the UAE is. They were fully aware that I was an experienced presenter and that I would be able to carry out the role well.

The job description was going to Ras Al Khaimah to start with and film there about how different the culture and life is in comparison to Dubai. It was also to convey how up and coming Ras Al Khaimah is as a place. It was a dream job! The other part of the job was to film in Dubai to show how thriving this part of the Emirates is and how it had become a central point for the world in every industry.

My heart sank that when I heard that we would have to go to Dubai even though almost a year had passed since my experience. I was healing at a steady pace however the scars were still there. It would be an amazing opportunity for me to showcase my skills as a presenter and travel at the same time. I have always been very passionate about travelling but I still needed some time to sleep over it.

The next day I received a message from the client to attend a meeting and discuss the project in more depth. I needed to make a decision quickly. What was I fearing and why? Besides, no one would be able to touch me because I would be going in a group and the majority of the shoot would be in Ras Al Khaimah! I had this constant battle with myself as to whether I should go or not. In the bigger scheme of things, I didn't have anything to lose as I was going for work and I would rarely be on my own, surely. This went on and on. I had to make a decision there and then! Feeling courageous and very brave I did it, I said yes! I was going!

I attended the meeting with my very good friend and manager at the time, Amar who has amazing negotiating skills, just to ensure everything was above board. No one dare say no to Amar! Everything was kosher. The meeting was most productive and exciting. I was reassured that they would look after me throughout. My manager was happy which meant I was happy. I also learnt that I would be working with a co presenter called Samara who was also a model and the daughter of a very famous international fashion designer. I was told not only is she easy on the eye but very easy going and a level-headed person. She sounded like the ideal colleague. However knowing what the industry people are like, I needed to meet her and judge her for myself!

CHAPTER 20

Every day I questioned myself as to whether I was doing the right thing by accepting the presenting job that was taking me back to the country where I lived in my worst nightmare. I couldn't forever live in this fear and so this was an opportunity for me to strengthen myself and face my demons straight on.

It took a good few days for me to calm myself down and embrace the adventure I was about to embark on. I had never been to Ras Al Khaimah and so was becoming intrigued with this part of the Emirates. I was looking forward to presenting and all the challenges I would have to face as a presenter. I still hadn't met Samara however a meeting was scheduled by the client for us to meet and get to know each other so that we would be able to interact more naturally on screen.

I needed to break the news to my family that I was heading to the UAE quite soon. It took some talking and a lot of reassuring but with a lot of persuasion they finally came round. Besides I was going on a work project with a team of professionals so I would not be on my own plus it was an amazing opportunity for my confidence and my career from all aspects. It was important to see all the positives! Feeling better that everyone was now aware of my plan of action, it was time to hit the road and head for the meeting with my co-host.

It was a beautiful clear day which made the drive so much more pleasant. I had my chill out music in the car. This became a ritual as it always calmed my nerves and put me on a good vibe. I parked my car in the car park and walked into the lobby of the hotel where we would all be meeting. It was a convenient location for all of us. I spotted the client and headed towards him. Samara was there too. It was great to see her. She is so tall, beautiful and very posh. Everything that was said about her was most definitely true! She was very easy to chat to which helped and before long we were chatting like we had known each other a life time. I felt very comfortable in her company and knew that we would have a real blast. After getting to know each other a little better, we had brief conversations about the project and that was it, meeting over. The next time we would be seeing each other would be at the airport. Most of the team were heading out before. Only Samara and I would be travelling out together.

I had done my shopping a few days prior to the meeting. Whilst shopping it dawned to me that I was going to Dubai. That weird uncomfortable feeling kept disturbing me. One minute I was completely fine about going, the next I was overloaded with all the doubts and negativity. I had come so far in every way and so thought it best to go with it and take each moment at a time! I really wanted to buy a gift for Maher and keep it with me just in case I was able to meet up with him. It would be amazing to surprise him. He had been there for me at my time of need. The sad thing was that his number had changed and so I wasn't able to keep in contact. He had proved himself as a true friend. There are very few people in this world that are that genuine. I really was hoping that we would meet. I could always go to his shop to see if he was still working there. It would be worth a try for sure.

It also came down to the simple fact as to whether I would be comfortable and confident to go out and about in Dubai. No point in worrying myself silly about it now. Best to deal with it nearer the time!

The main thing I needed was sun block and some casual summer clothing as it was going to be hot! My suitcase was compact in size and I managed to fit everything in comfortably. Unfortunately no one was available to take me to the airport so good old public transport it was. It wasn't too bad to be fair, just one change on the train which was manageable. I kept getting flash backs of when I was going to Dubai and when I came back for my things but then I cut the thoughts dead. I had to be harsh with myself. I was not going to fall back into that pit of misery and depression. I wasn't going to allow myself to at any cost!

I put on my music and enjoyed the views for the rest of my train journey. I dragged my luggage off the train and headed towards the departure lounge. The airport was heaving. I began to feel a bit flustered with the sea of people before me. I took my phone out of my pocket to call Samara to see if she had reached there yet. Just as I dialled her number I saw her wave at me a few yards down from where I was standing. There she was, tall as ever with her long locks loose, looking even more stunning than before. She was hard to miss.

We checked in our luggage and made our way to duty free. She was a serious shopper and was not going to let an opportunity like this slip away. We carried on from where the point of where we had left! We were both chatting and giggling away like school children. It was going to be a fun trip for sure.

After a little look around the shops we made our way to the gate as our flight was boarding. It was nice to have some good company on the flight for a change.

It was a night flight to Dubai and miraculously we managed to get a bit of sleep on the way. The plan of action was that the project manager was going to pick us up from Dubai Airport and then we would be driven to Ras Al Khaimah. Samara had never been to the UAE and was so excited. I on the other hand had a good healthy slice of experience of being in the UAE. There was no way I was going to tell her anything apart from the fact that I had been to Dubai before. Nothing more! It wasn't necessary!

It felt so weird being back at Dubai Airport. The sensation that was running through my body was unique and most uncomfortable. I couldn't speak much so kept the conversation to a minimum. It was like I had switched to mute mode. I held it in without showing any signs of discomfort on my face. We walked briskly to the exit of the airport doors and there in front of us was the project manager with the driver who took our luggage as I dived into the vehicle. My heart beat had been racing crazily from the time I stepped off the plane to this point. It was natural for that would happen. After all, it was my first time back in Dubai after that horrifying ordeal! I was so glad that we wouldn't be staying in Dubai just yet.

I calmed myself down and diverted the conversation towards the project and what we would be doing. This was truly consoling as the excitement as to why I was there began to kick in. Forty minutes later, we had arrived at our spectacular hotel. It was lavish beyond belief and had all the trimmings and more. Samara and I were given our very own cute little villa. I was totally gob smacked as I opened the door to my new home for the next good ten days. It was stunning with so much space. It even had a separate living room. The décor was so tasteful and totally to my liking, minimal, simple, elegant and sophisticated. Now this was what I called living it up!

I was feeling quite tired and so decided to get some sleep. The plan was that we would all meet up in the lobby later to meet the rest of the crew and run through the schedule. The sleep had done me a world of good. I was so refreshed and appreciative of my surroundings. I was the last one to get to the meeting but it was fine as they were still on introductions. It was so nice to meet the film crew and learn that we weren't just working with anyone but crew members that had worked on major documentaries that I had actually seen on television.

We then worked our way through the schedule which was action packed with some fantastic features and locations. We had a driver that would take us around everywhere and would be at hand at all times. It was living the dream!

The most magical thing about this project was that I had to do things out of my comfort zone. On the first day of my shoot we went to a famous fish market where I was dared to kiss a shark! A dead one of course! I am not good with water but then had to swim in natural spring waters. It was an amazing experience as the water was so naturally warm. The most challenging shoot entailed me climbing a mountain. That was just for starters because then I had to climb a fort on top of the mountain. It didn't end there as then I had to then climb the roof of the fort and do my piece to camera in fifty degrees heat which was quite something considering I have a great fear of heights. I put mind over matter because I felt so much passion for what I was doing.

It was amazing stumbling across a cute little palace where apparently the Sheikh's have parties. The nice man looking after the palace let us in to have a nosy around. Needless to say we took full advantage of this and got some great pieces to camera. Another memorable memory was when we went to a shooting club. Shooting is a big sport in the Middle East. Prior to that I had never held a riffle! It weighed so much and I found it a bit difficult to hold on to it properly. When I was doing my piece to camera, it was hilarious how everyone jumped back because I had the riffle in my hand but no full control over it. I had a professional with me helping me so it was very safe.

In this scene I am seen taking a shot at my target. Thanks to camera trickery I hit the target beautifully. Of course in real life that was not the case! This trip really made me realize how fortunate I was to have this amazing opportunity. It became a turning point in my life and in my career. I loved being a presenter and felt that I would be most happy to do this till I was ninety years old! Providing I live that long of course! I was facing a lot of challenges and accomplishing them at the same time. Being a presenter defined me as a person and reassured me of my capabilities regardless of my fears. It was truly blissful!

Our time in Ras Al Kahimah had been most productive as we had filmed a lot of amazing mind blowing footage. I had learnt so much about the history and how it was developing so quickly. I even got to see the ruler of Ras Al Khaimah which was a huge bonus. I was beginning to really enjoying myself to the full.

I became so heavily involved in what I was doing that I didn't have time to think about anything negative which was a blessing!

Sadly our time in Ras Al Khaimah was coming to an end. I wished we could have stayed on for longer but unfortunately that would not have been possible as we needed to get some footage of Dubai. This part of the trip made me very nervous indeed. I had no idea how I would handle this. It was best to go with the flow. I had been very professional and strong so far. It was highly important to remain on that level.

I very reluctantly said good bye to my villa that I had made my home and become so attached to. Time for the second half of the adventure and so off we went with the driver to our next location, Dubai, my most dreaded place!

I was on edge throughout the short journey to Dubai. To be fair I had a good enough reason to feel this way but at the same time I knew I couldn't let it take over my life again. I hadn't done anything wrong after all! This would be the biggest test for me without a doubt. I avoided looking out of the window. The only good thing was that we were staying in a hotel resort that was located quite far down the main highway on Sheikh Zayed Road in Jumeirah. It was a beautiful hotel and equally lavish but I wasn't feeling the same feeling as before. I just wanted to get to my room as quickly as possible. Thankfully our rooms were ready. There wasn't a shoot planned on this particular day as the cameramen needed to go and check out some locations.

Samara and I decided that we would both unpack and then meet later. I had sorted through my things in no time and so decided to have a lie down. Just as my head hit the pillow, Samara phoned my room. She said that she had unpacked too and was ready to explore the city. I was getting palpitations! I was more than happy to chill by the pool all day even though normally this would not be my thing to do, not all day anyway. I didn't want to shop or see anything. I had seen enough of it all to last me a life time. The big question was how could I convince Samara not to go out? This was a difficult task as Dubai is notorious for shopping, one of Samara's biggest passions. It truly is a shopper's paradise. How do I get out of this one?

She came into my room and I made some tea. We binged on biscuits and then she asked me where the best place was to go shopping. The colour of my face had dramatically changed. I was stumbling over words. She knew there was something the matter as I was no longer was my jovial self.

It's like I became a different person in seconds and not the person she knew. All I wanted to do was stay in. This was not normal on any accounts! I resisted for as long as possible still trying to skirt around this uncomfortable situation but then eventually gave in. I decided that I couldn't hold it in anymore. I needed to come clean and so I started with my story and she listened with great intrigue and sadness especially when I told her how I had been treated. I didn't go as far as the sexual assault. I did not feel there was any reason to go down that route. Other than the doctor, nobody knew about it. That's the way I wanted it! She suggested we go to the main mall which was the one I used to go to a lot.

You can only but imagine how I felt at this point! She did say that if I felt uncomfortable or uneasy at any point, we would immediately return to the hotel. As scared as I was, I thought that was a fair deal. That aside I needed to confront my fear. After all, it wasn't Dubai itself that had harmed me but some evil people that weren't even locals and it was the thought of meeting them that freaked me out. It had to be now or I would always be scarred from this place. I plucked up the courage and agreed to the deal on offer. We got a taxi to the mall. I tried to remain calm in the car by talking about random things to divert my attention to the present situation. It was hard! The taxi parked up right near the main entrance. I felt my body get heavy.

It took me longer than normal to get out of the car but at least I got out. We made our way to the entrance doors of the mall. I took a deep breath and walked in. I managed to walk a few yards before my body refused to move. I froze on the spot. It was horrible but I just didn't have any control. Samara could see how much I was struggling and she felt so bad for me. I didn't want to let her down or myself. I had to do this for me!

Eventually I felt some life kick into me and I left the spot where I was stationed for what seemed like a very long time. I took a deep breath and walked. Samara still concerned asked me if I was ok. As we were walking round I began to relax and regain my confidence slowly. I was going to win this battle no matter what. That's what I kept saying to myself. I was really pushing myself to the full. My determination and willpower seemed to be paying off in spells. We stopped for some food. It then became about the food, the atmosphere and the weather which was a good thing. This helped me hugely. I was slowly pulling myself away from the negativity that I was giving so much attention too and learning to control it. For the rest of the day I was much more comfortable and managed to turn my attention to other things like all the attention Samara was getting from all the shoppers walking by.

They were intrigued by her because she has such presence and her personality that was glittering away so brightly. It was pure entertainment for me. That evening when we got back to our hotel, I was feeling so much lighter and better within myself. I had faced my worst fear. I was eternally grateful to Samara for having the confidence in me and helping me fight my demons.

We were filming some mind-blowing locations. I was beginning to see Dubai from a very different perspective. I was doing my job extremely well and was so proud! It was as natural as breathing for me. It seemed a bit more rushed in Dubai as time was more limited, however it was nice to have a day off to chill.

Both Samara and I received a note that had been pushed under the door. It was an invitation to go to a watch factory. We would be driven there and back plus receive a watch as a gift. There would be no obligation to buy. It was a win-win situation. We quickly had a scrumptious breakfast and waited in the lobby for our ride. I loved the attention to detail and the Arabian hospitality as we were picked up in a swanky Mercedes on time. Whilst in the car I wanted to ask Samara if she wouldn't mind accompanying me to see Maher. She was fully in the picture as to who he was. She was more than happy to join me. This meant a lot. She also said that she had been meaning to ask me something for some time. I was very intrigued. She wanted to know if I had had my lips pumped up. She had noticed that my lips were quite full from when I first met her and that she had been having conversations with the project manager about this. I burst into fits of laughter. Seeing me laugh in such hysterics got her going too. It was a hilarious moment. Once I regained my sanity I told her that I hadn't and that a lot of people always assumed that I had interfered with my lips. I was naturally blessed! What more could I say? I took it as a compliment of course!

We got to the watch factory and were treated like king and queen on arrival. Something I could get used to very easily! We were escorted to a private showroom where the gentleman displayed a collection of very different watches. I had a phenomenal collection of watches and was looking to see if anything caught my eye to add to my collection. They were nice but not quirky enough for me. He then showed us the watch that they would give us for free. It was a sleek yet simple Swiss watch. They asked if we wanted our photographs on the faces of the watches. Being modest we both agreed on having pictures of ourselves on them, as you do! Within a short space of time they were ready for us to take away.

It was such a pleasant experience stress free. We thanked them and headed back to the hotel. It was a lovely souvenir to take back.

I had bought Maher a designer t-shirt. He was quite into his clothes and appearance like a lot Lebanese people. It was the least I could do. It was a quick run up to the room whilst Samara waited in the lobby. I locked up and decided to walk down the stairs rather than use the lifts. It was a nice mini workout.

We jumped into a taxi and headed towards the mall where Maher worked. It was pot luck as to whether he was going to be there or not but it was worth the trip. There were some nice shops in the mall which I knew Samara would appreciate. She loved her bling and there were quite a few bling shops there. It felt strange stepping into that mall.

The last time I was there was when my life was a huge mess. I didn't know whether I was coming or going! I knew the mall well having been there several times before. As I got closer to the shop, my heart was all over the place. A lot of old memories were coming to the forefront of my mind. I was really hoping Maher would be there. It would be amazing for him to see how well I had progressed. I could see that the light was on in the shop. We both speeded up our pace. I opened the door and to my amazement, there he was! He couldn't believe his eyes. He gave me hug. I introduced Samara to him and he gave her a big hug too. He was genuinely so happy to see me in a better state. There was so much to catch up on!

He was obviously very content and doing well in life which I was so happy to hear. We couldn't just leave it there so he told us to have a walk around the mall and to come back in an hour. We would all be going for dinner that evening. That was a fantastic idea. So, we went to have a good look around. I made some recommendations for shops. It had been very productive as we both me and Samara made some purchases. An hour zoomed by and so off we went back to Maher's shop. He had just finished closing up. He suggested a restaurant with great views of the water. We were both immediately sold.

He was so right about the restaurant. It had mind blowing views, so tranquil and peaceful, a perfect location to spend quality time. The great thing about Samara was that she got on with everyone. She was a good laugh and enjoyed life to the ultimate. Everyone loved her company. We ordered a mezze which was beautifully arranged on the giant plate. It tasted as good as it looked. The conversations were kept light and positive. I was telling Maher how I was excelling in my career.

My family had sent well wishes his way for all he had done for me. They were eternally grateful. I pulled out the bag which had the t-shirt folded in neatly. I handed it over to him. He was so overwhelmed. It was the best purchase I had made. The evening could not have been more perfect! It was getting late and so Maher very kindly dropped us off to our hotel. I took his new number so that we could stay in touch. I was so glad we had taken the risk and come to the mall. It had been so worth it!

Just as we were getting out, I randomly asked him if he had heard anything about Luca, as after all, he had been Maher's neighbour back in Lebanon. I was sad to hear that Luca's father was seriously ill; after all I couldn't blame the father for having such an evil child! I also learnt that Luca was living a life of hell and misery and that he was forced to work in the mines. The word karma came to mind immediately. I must admit that this gave me a huge amount of joy and satisfaction. He deserved every bit of it! He had earned this. He had messed up so many people's lives. It was time he had a taste of his own medicine. What goes around comes around for sure.

There were only two more nights left in Dubai. I was letting my hair down and enjoying myself. It was well deserved. I had also made a great friend in Samara. Things were looking up. This trip had helped me in more ways than one and I was so appreciative of this opportunity. It was the best type of therapy that I needed in order for me to close this chapter once and for all. I felt like I was slowly bonding with this city again!

CHAPTER 21

Back in the UK and I was feeling a bit restless. I was evaluating my trip in more depth. It had not only been successful work wise but also quite special in terms of helping me with my confidence, my outlook on life and my appreciation of life. I was most certainly in a better place. I also felt that I was ready for a change. I needed a new challenge. I had always toyed with the idea of moving to London but never put it into practice. It made sense to move because I was in London a lot for work. Sometimes twice a week!

The commuting was too tiring, time consuming and way too expensive. Moving to London would have a lot of advantages like the fact that I would be able to do last minute bookings which was always the case and that I would be in the hub of the media industry. Not to forget the diversity London has as I love to meet people from all different backgrounds. Naturally I would be careful as to who I choose to make friends with. It would be a huge transaction but then I felt the timing was right. The trip had inspired me and got me thinking about a lot of things.

That night I spoke with my friend Shahin and I just dropped it into conversation that I had this wild thought of moving to London. She encouraged it and said that it was impeccable timing as she knew of someone who was close to her who had a spare room going cheap. I would only have to share the whole house with one person. This was ideal as I was not used to sharing so having to share with one person would help ease me in. I instantly made a decision and said that I would take the offer. This all happened within a week literally. I was actually moving to London! What a spontaneous decision! At least it was a place that I was familiar with. I didn't particularly like London because all I used to see was tubes and stairs. This way I would be able to explore the city more, get to know it even better and be available for work any time! It made so much sense.

I broke the news to my family, telling them that I needed a change and that the move would help my career and me as a person. Surprisingly they were very understanding and respected my decision. Shortly after breaking the news of wanting to move to London, I told them that I would be going at the end of the week. Another shock for them to endure in a short space of time! As expected the news was a massive blow. It was all happening very quickly. Just the way I like it. I do not believe in wasting time. If anything needs to be done, it needs to be done there and then as tomorrow never comes!

It just so happened that I was moving to London on Eid day. I remember so vividly loading up my car with all my belongings. I was taking only all the essentials. All my family were going to meet in Manchester at one of my aunt's house. She was cooking Eid dinner for us all. It was nice as this would mean that I would get to see everyone before heading off to the big smoky city! It was going to be a huge change for me but I was more than ready for this challenge. Whilst having dinner, I got a bit over excited by all the variety of delicious food that lay in front of me and I insisted on trying everything. It was obvious the normal me was back bigger and stronger as my love for food was blooming like never before. I most certainly had eaten way more than what I could handle as I was bulging out left right and centre. It was worth it! It would be true to say I would have to do a very healthy amount of exercise to shift all that I had consumed in such a small amount of time!

I didn't want to leave too late, so started saying my goodbyes knowing full well that would take a good whack of time! I did feel very sad to be leaving my family. I was never good at saying goodbyes. I wanted to avoid getting too emotional. It would just make it that much harder. So I did my rounds as swiftly as possible and got into the car. It was going to be a long drive down without a doubt! Thank God for my amazing collection of sounds! This northerner was about to become a southerner!

The great thing about me is that I never got home sick and so always settled into my new surroundings very quickly. London initially sure was a culture shock for me with the craziness on the tubes and the lack of etiquette people showed. No one opened doors for me. There was rarely a *'please'* or *'thank you'*. Lots of miserable faces wherever you looked. The biggest shock to my system was when I saw a sign in the window of an estate agent's office next to a tube station saying not to ask for any directions! Welcome to London! Of course not everyone in London is like that, however it did became a case of; if you can't beat them join them!

With that in mind it was not long before my southern side was coming out in its full glory! I soon was getting very frustrated with tourists taking their own sweet time on the stairs of tubes, on the high streets and everywhere, especially when I was running late for a casting or job. The thing in London is that you have to allow so much time to get to your destination. They can be all sorts of obstacles in your way like engineering works on the tubes which means you have to take the scenic route, providing tubes are running.

If not then trying to find the right buses that will take you to where you need to get to eventually bearing in mind having to deal with the other millions of people who are in the exact same situation as you! It is a different world altogether! The pace of life in London is unbelievably insane. Up north you can do ten things in a day and still have time for yourself, whereas in London you do one thing and the day is over. It's an extreme contrast of lifestyles.

I was very appreciative of being able to do last minute modelling jobs which tends to happen a lot in this industry. You could be fast asleep in bed and the phone will ring asking to see if you can do a shoot an hour later. It has happened to me on several occasions. Luckily I have been able to work at the last minute. More work more money! After all London is where it all happens. It is one of the most vibrant cities in the world.

I was beginning to appreciate this reasonably soon which is a very positive thing as I don't think I would have survived otherwise. There is always something to do in London no matter what you are in to. Every culture has its own hideout.

It's so diverse and wonderful. You rub shoulders with people from all corners of the world on a daily basis. The best thing is that there is no chance of you being stranded. Unfortunately up north there is no public transport after 11pm so you either take a very long walk or get a taxi whereas in London there are always night buses to get you to any destination at anytime.

Before moving to London I had informed all my London model agencies that I was now more local to them and more available for work which was a great move as it wasn't before long they started pushing me out for work. I was meeting some amazing people with amazing tales to tell. I found that I was being more proactive in promoting myself and finding work off my own back too. I was taking a speculative approach to television and radio companies which paid off very soon as I landed my first TV presenting job with a very well-known Asian television company. I was presenting a music show. The great thing was that I wasn't cooped up in a studio instead I was always out and about at different locations and feeling the heart-beat of London.

It all went from there! I was very content in where I was staying. It was very comfortable and homely. Even though I have always had a very bad sense of direction, I was getting to know my way around quite well. I didn't think it would happen so soon but London was beginning to feel like my home because I was settling down at a good pace. It was a very positive feeling.

My main goals now were to be successful in my career and enjoy life to its full, to take each day as a blessing and be fully appreciative for everything I have. It truly is amazing how small the world is. I never used to believe this before but since moving to London, my outlook on this saying has taken a different turn. I got to know a lot of people very quickly but for me it's about quality not quantity.

I have always had a habit of exchanging people's contact numbers who I felt connected with in some way and managed to actually keep in touch with them. I find it most satisfying to see how well people are progressing in their lives.

I met one of my very good friends on a shoot. It was quite a funny situation. I was on a two day job with beautiful international looking models. It was like the United Nations crowd. Models from all corners of the world! Whilst on lunch break I could hear this one particular model that was very excited and loud. I turned around and I saw this very stunning model with Middle Eastern looks. Wasn't long before we were chatting and giggling! On the second day of the shoot we were practically inseparable. She's a live wire Turkish girl called Mine Akkus, a much sorted girl with a great sense of humour. Not to forget beautiful of course. We kept in touch and that was it. We became best friends to the point where I was a witness at her registry wedding and attended her wedding ceremony in Istanbul. I love the randomness of life!

This one particular day I had an audition at a national radio station. As per usual I was there early. It was refreshing that the atmosphere was not of an intense meat market but rather of a selected crowd. I walked towards the receptionist who smiled a fake smile. She took all my necessary details then pointed me out to the seating area. I could not believe how quiet it was. There were only two people ahead of me. Fingers crossed this was going to be a quick one. I hated all the unnecessary waiting around. It was always worse when going for modelling work.

As I got cosy in my seat I started to make conversation with the person sat on my left. It was a great way to get to know people. We got chatting and weirdly enough this person that I was talking to worked with my mums first cousin at Heathrow Airport. London is a huge place and the chances of that happening are quite slim but there you go! He came across as a very friendly, genuine and a pleasant guy who lived in west London. His name was Aman Gill. He was very passionate about both his jobs. He had great balance.

It felt like we had we known each other for a very long time which was nice, because some of the people that I would meet at castings would be more interested in my contacts and how they could benefit from knowing me. It felt good to discuss our views of the industry and how it would be better with people like us in it!

It was obvious to say we made an effort to keep in touch and so became good friends. Through Aman I have been most fortunate to meet some amazing people who I have become very close to and feel very comfortable with. They are more like my family than my friends. After knowing Aman for some time and realising that he equally has a crazy sense of humour, it was time to put our heads together and grace the media industry with something unique. Within a short space of time we landed a double-headed radio show that had extreme edge and quirkiness. Its rawness and realness wowed the audiences and took them to another level. Mission accomplished!

London is officially my home now and has been for some time. I love the vibe of this city and appreciate being surrounded by all the art, culture and all the wonderful things this city has to offer. It most certainly is a city that doesn't sleep! I have been blessed with amazing friends whom I trust with my life. They are always there for me no matter what. They are my tower of unconditional support and an inspiration to my life! They have restored the fact that there are still good humans in the world and that you can trust!

My confidence has soared in all directions to the point where I have returned to Dubai on several occasions for holidays and assignments. That brief feeling of negativity faded away some time ago. Dubai was never to blame. My relationship with Dubai was like a marriage. I married, I divorced, I loved, and I remarried!

I feel that I have lived many dreams and many nightmares. I still dream of living abroad specifically in Italy where I am seduced by the culture, the people, the food, the life! Its unpretentious elegance and natural beauty has taken me in its wings. I long for the day to be living there absorbed in my writing, watching the world go by in the Tuscan hills! It's good to dream and escape as only you can make it happen. Believe in yourself. Normally we only have one shot in life. I was blessed with a second chance and have made full use of it. I have learnt many lessons the hard way but I have still learnt at a huge cost.

It has made me very strong and determined and allowed me not to let anything get in my way.

I feel a huge sense of pride by having written this book. When you think about it deep, it's massive! Slowly slowly I am ticking off my to-do list. My next mission is to launch my unique collection of unisex accessories which I am very excited about so watch this space!

I visit my family as much as possible. Every moment with them is so precious and treasured. Their unconditional love is my fuel for my continued success. I just wish I could spend a lot more time with them rather than these flying visits that I just about manage to squeeze in here and there. I guess that's life. The key thing is to appreciate that the glass is half full rather than half empty and make the most of everything you have. Life is a wonderful gift. Embrace it with open arms and leave your dent in the world whatever that may be!

Be true to others, be true to yourself. Everything in life has a reason. What may seem wrong at the time may unfold to be the biggest right. We all have tales, we all have adventures. We all are right, we are all wrong, we get kicked down, and we get pulled up. Embrace the lows; embrace the highs because WHAT BREAKS YOU MAKES YOU!

Between the Lines

This little bonus section is something that I really wanted to share with you all. It's a peek at the 'behind the scenes' of my glamorous life whilst writing this book. It has been a challenge and a half. I officially started writing on 3rd April 2017 and finished on 7th August 2017. The idea for this book had been brewing in my head for a good few years. I guess the timing wasn't right and I was not physically ready to revisit this part of my past life.

I had previously only managed to write about two lines before stopping it all together. I decided to rest it for a while until I was ready to continue. Whilst writing I switched off from the outside world completely which meant no socialising with friends or even going out for castings and modelling jobs. One day when I needed to go out to the post office to post an important letter down, I stepped outside, my eyes started to squint! The bright sunshine was hurting my eyes. I love the sun so for me this was a very weird experience. It truly was about being completely focused and had I not been so focused it would not had been possible to write this book. Discipline is a great skill!

Some days I would see the sun peeking through the net curtains but that's all I got. I didn't go to the gym or anywhere. The most exercise I got was walking to the bathroom upstairs and to the kitchen. I was practically living out of a room. I had exhausted every single episode of 'Come Dine with Me' as I found watching cooking shows was easier on the eye whilst typing. The sound was on mute of course. This didn't help too much as my attention turned to food. I would be literally be drooling about what I was going to be eating every few hours. It was blasphemous for me to just have a main course; it always had to be followed by a desert and several snacks in between. I am heavier in weight but thankfully it doesn't show too much. My attire was t-shirt, pyjamas and flip flops; very sleek for a model. I didn't even have time to shave on most days and so let my beard run wildly on my face.

How can I forget the sore bottom? Sitting on the same chair in the same position everyday! Not a great feeling!

There were times when I would enjoy remembering some of my happiest moments in the book but then there were times where I was reliving the nightmare, feeling the pain as if it were so fresh and raw! What I have learnt about myself is that how determined I actually I am. When I put my mind to something I see it through to the end no matter what.

I feel very proud to have achieved something so big. Writing a book of just over 70,000 words is quite special. Naturally on some days I would question whether I would ever finish it as my patience was wearing thin but I would also have days where I would write continuously for hours and lose track of time and where I was.

I have lost lots of sleep, and lost days of leisure with my friends and family to complete this project. It feels so surreal to have finally reached my destination. It has been an emotional rollercoaster ride but I have done it. I have written a book in what I consider to be a short space of time. I feel ecstatic! Anything is achievable if you put your mind to it!

A few words from the author

"I hope and pray that you find this book educational and inspiring and understand the positive message it's conveying which is when you reach rock bottom, the only way is up! I am the living proof of this! Have faith in yourself. We are a lot stronger than what we give ourselves credit for. We are all human, and make mistakes. Learn from your mistakes to better yourself. Love and trust, but be on your guard, not everyone thinks or feels the way you do! Life is to be enjoyed so enjoy it and live it to the max!

May you always be blessed with peace and happiness!

Much Love

Nadeem x

Contact The Author

Instagram: @nadeemahmeduk

Twitter: @Nadeemahmeduk

E Mail: doomedindubaibook@gmail.com